The
GLORY
of
HEAVEN

Other Books by Betty Malz

Angels by My Side
Making Your Husband Feel Loved
Morning Jam Sessions
My Glimpse of Eternity
Prayers That Are Answered
Simplicity
Super Natural Living
Touching the Unseen World
Women in Tune

The
GLORY
of
HEAVEN

Inspiring
TRUE STORIES
and ANSWERS *to*
COMMON
QUESTIONS

BETTY MALZ

Chosen
a division of Baker Publishing Group
Minneapolis, Minnesota

© 1989, 2013 by Betty Malz

Previously published as *Heaven: A Bright and Glorious Place*

Published by Chosen Books
11400 Hampshire Avenue South
Bloomington, Minnesota 55438
www.chosenbooks.com

Chosen Books is a division of
Baker Publishing Group, Grand Rapids, Michigan

Printed in the United States of America

Library of Congress Cataloging-in-Publication Data
Malz, Betty.
    [Heaven]
    The glory of heaven : inspiring true stories and answers to common questions / Betty Malz.
        pages cm
    Rev. ed. of: Heaven : a bright and glorious place. c1989.
    Summary: "Get a glimpse of eternity from breathtaking firsthand accounts as well as answers to common questions, including Where is heaven? and What will it be like?"— Provided by publisher.
    ISBN 978-0-8007-9559-7 (pbk.)
    1. Heaven—Christianity. I. title.
BT846.3.M335 2013
236′.24—dc23   2013023233

Cover design by Dual Identity, Inc.

13 14 15 16 17 18 19   7 6 5 4 3 2 1

This book is dedicated to
Sara Douglas

She has prayed for me for 28 years—while I travel, while I speak, while I write, especially daily while writing this book, *The Glory of Heaven.*

Sara celebrated Easter this year in the great Temple of worship, east of God's throne room, in the Holiest Place. She died the day before Easter. In God's overruling, practical, providential plan, she paid several weeks ago for the printing of a booklet, a mini-version of my personal resurrection story. We gave a copy to everyone who attended church Easter Sunday, while she lay in repose at the funeral chapel two blocks from our morning worship service.

You spell Sara "*love for others.*" She called me that Saturday and asked, "What may I pray for?" I gave her the names of two men who were ill. She prayed for them on the phone, then closed by praying for the editing and publication of this book. Then, in her usual manner, she ended the conversation with a high, sweet *Bye.* She never wasted her time or yours.

Her last words were prayers for others and for this book. Her husband and our friend, Lawrence, called to tell us that she hung up the phone, sat down at the table, and fell over onto the floor.

The day of her funeral I took down from the top shelf of my kitchen cabinet a small glass decanter I have kept there for 21 years. It contains a dime and two badly corroded pennies. Explanation: That day 21 years ago I desperately needed someone to pray with me. My husband had died following open heart surgery. My mother was facing terminal cancer, and my two-year-old daughter, April, had swallowed a dime and two pennies. X rays at Mease Hospital showed they were lodged in her sphincter muscle. After 22 days they still had not passed. April had a high fever, and was very sick from infection resulting from the corrosion of the coins. Doctors decided to operate at eight o'clock the morning of the 23rd day.

I called Sara to pray. "It's my birthday," I told her. "I can't bear the thought of my baby having surgery on my birthday."

She prayed, "Lord Jesus, our Great Physician, dislodge those corroded coins and cause them to pass." Before she said her usual quick *Bye*, she remarked to me, "You're going to have a happy birthday. It will be fun to see how God answers this prayer!" Two hours later the coins passed into the little white "throne" (her potty chair). No surgery necessary!

Sara considered prayer "fun" and talked about heaven with simple, childlike delight.

Like Sara, we should learn all we can about heaven, preparing even more than we would before making a trip to another country. After all, heaven is our future home—forever!

Contents

Acknowledgments

A nn Weinheimer and Jane Campbell at Chosen Books:
Ann, my editor and cheerleader; Jane, the "idea wizard"

Len LeSourd
Sharon and Lisa Huie
Bill Van Garven
Jennifer Stone
Ed Schlossmacher
Ed Tunkel
Roy "Chuck" Gates
Ethel Sipe
Karen Siddle

Debbie Daer
Paul Schurdell
Paul Priddy
Dwight Diller
Oden Hetrick
Elliot Hong
Charlie Messenger
Jack Cociloua
E.L. Cole

1

Unrealistic Realities

I t is not always easy to believe in something we cannot see. But unseen does not mean nonexistent. Scientists are ever searching the unexplored; children are born with a love for magic tricks; the middle aged chase rainbows; the elderly hope to avoid the unavoidable—death. Every human has an inborn yearning for the permanent, something lasting, eternal. It is the unexplainable hope of heaven. And that is the essence of faith.

Still, few things try our ability to believe in the unseeable the way heaven does. Heaven is the promise of all that is grand and glorious. It is the fulfillment of every dream. It is the place of everlasting joyful communion with our Lord Jesus Christ.

But we cannot see it. We can hardly even imagine it. How can we know for certain, down deep in our hearts, that it is the most wonderful place in all of creation, and that we as believers in Jesus Christ are headed there?

We learn about heaven most of all, naturally, from Scripture. The revelation given to John, for instance, gives us fascinating insight into the beautiful city, the New Jerusalem, and many events that will take place there. References throughout the Bible point to our ultimate destination and the lovely dwelling place of God.

We can learn in a corollary way about heaven from believers who had near-death experiences and recovered with vivid recollections of what they saw there—although we have to exercise great caution and discernment about what we hear, always checking it against Scripture as our final authority.

I have enjoyed talking about heaven ever since my own experience with death, which I wrote about in *My Glimpse of Eternity*. After suffering a ruptured appendix eleven days before surgery—followed by gangrene, pneumonia, a bowel block, collapsed veins and a coma—my heart finally stopped beating. Medical personnel removed the life-support system, covered me with a sheet and called my husband and parents.

I knew nothing of the happenings around my physical body during the next 28 minutes, for I felt as if I had gotten onto a roller coaster at Disney World. At the high point of the ride, the height of exhilaration, my body lurched with anticipation, and the only way I can describe what happened is to say that I was launched from this planet to another place. I was suddenly walking in a meadow of waving green grass among flowers of colors I had never seen before. I had arrived in the countryside of heaven. It was as real as Africa or America or any other earthly landscape we can walk upon.

I have never felt such belonging. Heaven is a reality! An unseeable, unsearchable reality—but reality nonetheless! Think about it. Many things that seem unrealistic are reality. We cannot see oxygen, but it is a reality.

Our friend Clyde Miller, who pastors a church in Cincinnati, preached a sermon on unrealistic realities such as those in the following list. These are things we have never seen, but would not deny are real. They are unseen, but they assuredly exist:

death	hate	life	health
energy	strength	fear	wind
peace	headaches	greed	depression
admiration	integrity	love	passion
faith	lust	joy	respect

The most *real* realities are the things of heaven. These shall endure while eternities roll. How important it is to set our minds and affections "on the things above, not on the things that are on earth" (Colossians 3:2)!

I chatted with a woman in the Tampa airport recently. She saw me reading my New Testament and remarked, "I'm a religious illiterate. For years I thought Joan of Arc was Noah's wife! But I know," she added more seriously, "that there's something after this life. I have never seen love, but I know it's real. I know there is a God, though I've never touched Him."

Dr. Richard Eby, who recorded his "heavenly" experiences in his popular book *Caught Up into Paradise*, described his initial reaction at seeing heaven this way:

> I felt suddenly at home. I was instantly no longer in a strange world as earth had seemed so often of late, but in Paradise, personally prepared for my arrival. I didn't need my glasses to see ten inches or ten miles. . . . I had no memory of earth or the fact that I had plunged from an upper balcony . . . head first, with a thud onto the cement below . . . and was [dead on arrival] at the hospital. In a twinkling of an eye, as quick as a wink or a blink, my mind and body were renewed exquisitely beyond imagination.
>
> I gasped with glee at God and His handiwork everywhere in everything. I was home at last. What a joy! There was no pain, just a presence of peace. I looked at myself in a translucent flowing gown, pure white. . . . I viewed the forests . . . and the valley floors were gorgeous, with four-petaled flowers on stems two feet tall with real gold at the centers. . . .

13

I looked for my wife. In the distance I heard her call, "Richard, Richard!" The lights went out and I was on the fourth floor of the hospital.

Dr. Petti Wagner said that in her experience, even though "I seemed to be walking on billowing white ether, there was firmness under my feet as I moved. . . . I felt twenty again, uninhibited. . . . Human words cannot express the flood of emotions and sensations."

Personally, I have often wondered why God allowed me, a born-again newspaper columnist born near Toad Hop, Indiana, former resident of North Dakota, now living in Florida, a second chance at life. I have never been to the Holy Land, but I think He may appoint me as a tour guide in the New Jerusalem since I *have* been there!

In fact, I have no idea why He allowed me to undergo the experience I did. Nevertheless, I believe that He has commissioned me and other "representatives of the resurrection" who have glimpsed the splendors of heaven to tell what is to come. We should "look not at the things which are seen, but at the things which are not seen; for the things which are seen are temporal, but the things which are not seen are eternal" (2 Corinthians 4:18). And the things that are eternal can be seen in this life only with the eyes of faith.

Remorse looks back; fear looks around; but faith looks up. When feelings fail, faith prevails. Our ultimate faith, of course, rests in Jesus Christ, who died on our behalf, rose again and is in heaven now preparing a place for us. We know it is true because He said so:

> "In My Father's house are many dwelling places; if it were not so, I would have told you; for I go to prepare a place for you. And if I go and prepare a place for you, I will come again, and receive you to Myself; that where I am, there you may be also."
>
> John 14:2–3

Job is a good example of faith in action. He was a respected and mature man. God said, "Consider him." When Job lost his possessions, his children and his health, he knew what it cost to hold on to faith. Even his wife suggested that he curse God and die so she could be freed from her misery. (What a miserable "helpmeet"!)

But Job persisted. He waited patiently in the gap between the things he understood and the things he did not understand. God did not reward him for suffering, but for holding on when he had no answers.

"Where is the place of understanding?" Job asked. "It is hidden from the eyes of all living. . . . God understands its way; and He knows its place. For He . . . sees everything under the heavens" (Job 28:20–21, 23–24).

And in this oldest book in the Bible, our friend Job—with neither New Testament nor Christian books to draw from—nevertheless declared: "I know that my Redeemer lives, and that in the end his will stand upon the earth. And after my skin has been destroyed, yet *in my flesh* I will see God" (Job 19:25–26, NIV, emphasis added).

We, too, must refuse to let things we do not understand rob us of what we believe. We must hold on to the hope of heaven and know that its unspeakable glories await us.

You might have a head start in claiming this hope if you have had a loved one die. That experience seems to give us a personal connection or investment there.

An old minister friend of ours lives with his wife near the Wabash River. He said they used to sit each morning with cups of coffee and remark casually about happenings on the other side of that river. Then their last daughter got married and moved with her husband to that other side. Now they love to look out over the river because people they love live there.

He said that it was the same with his feelings about heaven. He used to preach funerals with some detachment. After three of his children died, however, he suddenly took great interest in heaven in anticipation of the time he will go there to join them.

To reach heaven ourselves we must first die, of course, and that can be a frightening thought. We will talk about death more in the next chapter, but let's just say here that death is one of those realities that we can understand only in part because we have witnessed it, but have not experienced it. Yet with faith we can believe that death is the open door to the *best* of life—the infinite.

I have a hard time trying to picture that word *infinite*. A Princeton scientist, for example, says that the atom cannot be completely broken down. It is infinite, endless energy. Another scientist says he believes in an immortal soul because science has proved that nothing can disintegrate into nothingness, so we ourselves must be immortal.

Assuming this is true, that we will live forever—which, of course, is what the Bible teaches—can create hunger in believers for that eternal dwelling place. Reading the Bible can heighten our hope in the unseen reality of heaven. Realizing that Jesus lives there and we will walk in communion with Him is enough to burst our hearts with joy!

Do you have needs here? They will be met in heaven. Does your heart long for peace? reconciliation? truth? justice? All our longings will be fulfilled there in the light of Jesus' love.

In fact, there are many longings that can be met *only* in the reality of heaven. I will never forget the enormous sense of total fulfillment I felt as I walked along in that countryside toward the light of the city. The happiness I had enjoyed on earth compared to the happiness I felt in heaven was like comparing a forty-watt lightbulb to the sun.

I once interviewed a famous writer. When our conversation moved to the topic of fulfillment he confessed, "I should be the happiest man alive. I have a good wife, five good children, darling grandchildren and a contract for my next book. But I have restlessness deep inside me."

"I know that feeling," I told him. "During the most important times of my life—on my wedding day, when my children were born, when I played my best organ recital, wrote my best column, lived my most shining hour—I had a corner of melancholy in the hidden recess of my soul that was still not quite satisfied."

During my death experience, while I was walking up that hill toward those gates, which were pearl as described in the book of Revelation, I was suddenly completely fulfilled. I was arriving at the place I had been drawn to since the day I was born. I knew that I could do things there I could never do on earth, and that I would become there what I had always longed to be.

I believe that the inability to find fulfillment in this life—the quality that makes fulfillment an unrealistic reality—acts as an anchor to forever, a bridge to eternity so that we will not settle down too comfortably here. St. Augustine referred to the restlessness in every human being that is satisfied only in God. Billy Graham refers to the God-sized vacuum inside every person. This tug helps us transfer our affections from the temporary, in which we desire fulfillment, to the permanent, in which that reality of fulfillment is found at last.

And this "earthly tent" (2 Corinthians 5:1) in which we experience daily life is indeed temporary. Scripture says:

> It is a story: "We spend our years as a tale that is told" (Psalm 90:9, KJV).

> It is a pilgrimage: "We are sojourners before Thee, and tenants" (1 Chronicles 29:15).

> It is short-lived: "My days [are as short] as handbreadths" (Psalm 39:5).

> It is transient: "You are just a vapor that appears for a little while and then vanishes away" (James 4:14).

It is fragile: "Like a flower [man] comes forth and withers" (Job 14:2, KJV).

It is ephemeral: "All flesh is grass, and . . . grass withers" (Isaiah 40:6–7).

Our lives are brief, as is the memory of them in the eyes of future generations. We can try to immortalize ourselves, but writing our names in earth's books is like writing them in the sand at the beach. The next tide will swoosh them away. To be perpetual they must be recorded on the permanent monuments in heaven. Just think: Your name was written in that unseen realm when you first chose to believe!

Even though our lives are short, we have enough time to meet Jesus. He said that if we believe in Him, we will not die in our sins (see John 8:24). "Every one who calls on the name of the Lord shall be saved" (Acts 2:21). Our names will be written in the Book of Life in that unseen realm: "He who overcomes shall thus be clothed in white garments; and I will not erase his name from the book of life, and I will confess his name before My Father, and before His angels" (Revelation 3:5; see also Philippians 4:3; Revelation 20:15).

I have read that in the courtrooms of China are two books. When individuals are tried for certain crimes and found innocent their names are written in the book of life. If they are found guilty, their names are written in the book of death. Similarly, every person here now on earth either has his name recorded in the Lamb's Book of Life or does not. Every person is heading for either eternal joy with Jesus or eternal damnation, separated from His presence and, thus, from everything good.

A young woman wrote me about her uncle's stubborn refusal to believe in the reality of salvation or heaven. He was dying but had a miraculous recovery after believers prayed for him.

His doctor teased him that "the guys with the horns came after you, and I told them they couldn't have you!"

The uncle snorted, "I could believe in those streets of gold if I wanted to, but I think it's nonsense."

A dying man rarely lies.

Be honest in what you believe. Perhaps you are reading this and finding the reality of heaven hard to imagine. Or perhaps you think there is a heaven but you are not sure you are going there when you die.

Even if you cannot imagine the splendors of heaven, you can ensure your arrival there by believing in the One who paved the way for you. It is Jesus' home. Listen when He talks about it. John 8:51 tells us that Jesus said, "If anyone keeps My word he shall never see death." What a bargain! We can be born again into a new life with Jesus. We can be assured that He has opened the way to heaven and is preparing a place just for us. We can cling to the unrealistic reality of heaven.

I have received letters from people in other countries of the world who do not have freedom of worship, even though they are allowed to attend church services run by the government. Yet these people rejoice that they have been born again by reading the Bible—maybe even just a page torn from the Bible—or a Gospel tract.

Whether you are a movie star or a peasant, you will experience death. You can have victory over death by believing in Jesus: "'O death, where is your victory: O death, where is your sting?' The sting of death is sin, and the power of sin is the law; but thanks be to God, who gives us the victory through our Lord Jesus Christ" (1 Corinthians 15:55–57). You can be assured of this not by the light of reason but by God's revelation. We receive the gift of faith poured into our hearts by the Holy Spirit (see Acts 10:45; Romans 5:5; 12:3).

I received a letter from a woman in Florida last year who told how she had been suffering from pneumonia. While in the hospital, a nurse gave her a copy of my book *Angels by My Side* and said she would pray for her when she got home that night. The woman said that during the night an angel came into her room and offered this strange message: "There is life, warmth and breath." The woman believed immediately, put her faith in Jesus, experienced the new birth and recovered her health quickly.

Generally we are not aware of the unseen heavenly realities we call angels, which are commissioned by God to help us. Nor do we usually see the unseen forces that work against us, trying to cause us to lose our faith. The Bible says that Satan has made himself our prosecuting attorney. He is accusing you and me "before our God day and night" (Revelation 12:10; see also Zechariah 3:1–2).

But if we believe that Jesus died for us and that repenting for our sins means we are washed in the cleansing power of His blood, then we have Jesus as our Advocate, our Attorney, our Counsel for the Defense before His Father in heaven's court. No wonder Isaiah calls Him Wonderful Counselor and the Prince of Peace!

Can you accept the reality of what the Bible says? If you have not already done so, please pray to Jesus and accept Him as your Savior. Make that reality a part of your life. Pause now and pray this prayer:

Father, I know that "all have sinned and fall short of the glory of God" (Romans 3:23). I know, too, that "the wages of sin is death, but the free gift of God is eternal life in Jesus Christ our Lord" (Romans 6:23).

I now confess with my mouth that Jesus is Lord and believe in my heart that You raised Him from the dead (see Romans 10:9). By Your power and grace I claim that salvation is mine.

Thank You, Jesus, for saving me. Holy Spirit, come dwell within me and be my Teacher as I learn about the unrealistic realities of heaven, my forever home.

We get a sense sometimes around Christians that thinking about death is almost an act of forsaking one's faith—that it clouds our optimism and joy. It is true that the world is preoccupied with glamour, sports, health clubs, youth and wealth. Contrary to popular opinion, Vail, Colorado, is not heaven—even though there are no cemeteries there, and I saw one grocery store that displayed sixteen brands of caviar. Clearwater Beach, where I live, is not paradise either, although some choose to believe so! (My motto for life is: Anything worth doing is worth doing outdoors. My husband, Carl, has a motto for life, too: Anything worth doing is worth doing fast!)

Earthly realities will prove, ultimately, to fade away. But life after death is real. You did not choose to be born, but you can choose—and help others choose—to live a real life in heaven after this earth phase converts over to forever.

I suspect that many Christians fail to witness to others because they are not convinced themselves of the awesome reality of the afterlife—either heaven or hell. Think of it like this: Are you married? You never answer that question, "I think so" or "Perhaps." Regardless of your emotions on the subject, you are either married or single. So with the question of being saved and going to heaven. It is so easy that some miss it. I have met people who are too smart to understand.

Last night at bedtime I pulled a verse written on a card from our "Promise Box" of Scriptures. It was Psalm 19:1: "The heavens are telling of the glory of God." Then I went to the sliding glass door in our bedroom and looked for the stars. I thought we must be experiencing some fog outside since I could not see the sky clearly. Not until daylight when the sun came up did I realize our glass door was covered with dust from a windstorm! After washing it I could see out clearly.

Just so, we are to keep our hands clean and our hearts pure if we are to see Jesus' love, saving grace and eternal home.

Heaven is real, more real than any place you have ever been. And if you have accepted Jesus as your Savior, not only will you walk through those splendid gates one day, but each step you take today is actually a step on the road to eternity.

Sound unreal? Undoubtedly! But as soon as we are willing to grasp the reality of heaven, we can start to consider that ultimate destination with joy and wonder.

We are bound to have a lot of questions along the way. Will we recognize our loved ones? Will we have bodies? Will children who died on earth be adults in heaven? What about rewards and houses and recreation? By studying Scripture and listening to accounts from those who have had near-death experiences, I have come to believe that God delights in revealing to us some of the wonders awaiting us there.

I have interviewed 103 people who have had a close encounter with death, have died and returned to life or have had a vision of heaven. They range in age from five years old to 92. Our next chapter, "Death: A Point of View," approaches this topic from this vast age span, a full keyboard in its range and perspective. One need not be old to die or to contemplate the next life. I am amazed at the number of letters I receive about this that are written in crayon by children.

As Spurgeon recommended, "Lay hold on eternal life. It is a thing of the future and it is a thing of the present."

Let's look at some of the answers that will help us "lay hold on" this unrealistic reality.

2

Death: A Point of View

British historian Arnold Toynbee noted that Americans tend to say someone *passed on* or *passed away* instead of *died*. This gives the impression of trying to avoid death, even the mention of it. To some of us death is something to fear. To others it means oblivion, the end of life and the beginning of nothingness. To still others it marks a time of reunion and celebration. To all of us it is inevitable.

Have you wondered what it will feel like to die? I read in a book by George Maloney, S. J., *The Everlasting Now*, about the findings of two doctors who studied approximately a thousand cases of people at the point of death. They came up with an "average" description of what a prepared person experiences on his or her way out of life into what we know as death. This is what they wrote:

> When your heart stops and the hour of death comes, you will not break up and disintegrate like ice in the rapids of a river. Instead, it will be like diving into a new kind of reality. You will feel good and be happy in a very special way—"the peace which passeth all understanding." The weariness, the pain, and the sadness all will be left with the sheets on the hospital bed. You

23

will "light up from within" and then you will see someone warm and caring waiting to receive you. If your own close relatives are suitable for the task—and you for them—one will "pop in" as lifelike and loving as when you last saw him. But there will be a strange air of serenity around him. . . .

Something mild but powerful will envelop you. It will feel like the best moment of your life . . . you might have to grope for words—sacred, light, love. Neither one will really do, but you will feel it in the core of your being. . . .

The heartrending anguish of weeping relatives will appear to be childish and beside the point. Your own grand concerns—the unfulfilled dreams of the future, duties to loved ones, work, everything you ever looked forward to—will become small and unimportant, fading like dried flowers. With a sudden wave of joy, you will be ready to go.

My Aunt Gwen's point of view is that death is nothing to be feared. She just turned seventy and concludes that an old body is like an old house: "After fifty it's just scrape, paint and patch! The lucky ones are the ones already in heaven with all those repair bills behind them."

I asked my oldest daughter, Brenda, for her point of view. She is 35, married and has two darling children. She told me: "Years ago, as a little kid, I was frightened by death and heaven because they represented 'the end.' I was at the beginning point in my life with lots to look forward to. Papaw [her grandfather] would preach and say some people couldn't wait to get to heaven. It made me wonder if my wishing heaven could wait a little longer made me a poor Christian. Yet history shows that revival—and longing for the life to come—usually accompanies tough times like war and depression. The pre-Civil War slaves, for instance, couldn't wait for heaven because their lives were so miserable. John 3:16 says God loved the world. We should look forward to heaven but love the journey, too."

My point of view about death has changed, too. Looking back I remember when I was about five years old how my little brother Don and I would misbehave in church. Invariably Mother would whisper, "When we get home I have a score to settle with you." In my child heart I would pray, "Jesus, come quickly—before we get home."

Later, as Don and I began to participate—we sang; he played his saxophone, I my accordion; we quoted Scripture; we led in prayer before the offering was taken or at the close of the service—we paid attention. We were involved and enjoying ourselves and, eventually, I stopped asking Jesus to come quickly.

That desire changed once more after my own death experience. Even though I enjoy my life fully, I have an inner longing to regain the sense of fulfillment awaiting me there.

Circumstances can change our perceptions of death, as can a newfound desire to experience heaven. I believe that having anticipation for heaven is a healthy attitude, not an escapist one. We are certainly meant to enjoy life, but as I mentioned in the last chapter there is fulfillment we can find only in heaven.

Dr. Paul Walker and his wife, Carmelita, found her father's Bible shortly after his funeral. In the front he had written: "Death is the King's porter to usher in His guest."

Jesus said, "Do not be afraid; I am the first and the last, and the living One; and I was dead, and behold, I am alive *forevermore*, and I have the keys of death and of Hades" (Revelation 1:17–18, emphasis added). He also told us: "Because I live, you shall live also" (John 14:19).

Each moment of Jesus' earthly life was a preparation for His death. For us, too, each choice made along life's way must be done with free spirit for the good pleasure of our Father (see John 8:29).

Do you remember that Christ has conquered and set you free from "the law of sin and of death" (Romans 8:2)? And

25

that death has no sting for the redeemed ones (see 1 Corinthians 15:55–57)?

Even though the Bible says that death is "the last enemy that will be abolished" (1 Corinthians 15:26), in light of what Jesus has done for us, we do not have to fear it. Nor should we long for it, because our heavenly Father has a purpose for our lives that He wants to fulfill.

Death As a Doorway

Is death to you friend or foe? Do you think of death as the end of this life or the beginning of a new one? I prefer to think of death for the believer in Jesus Christ as a doorway, with obedience on this side and fulfillment on the other. Here are eight aspects of the fulfillment I believe we will find by walking through that doorway.

The End of Suffering and Pain

A man in Mississippi mailed me a yellowed page torn from an old book containing the vision of the owner of a cotton plantation during his dying hours:

> I see a slave arrive on the shore of the River of Life. He is met by joyous angels, and says, "I cannot take it all in. It is too much for these eyes! On earth I had no window, no rug in my old cabin, no picture on my wall, no flower in the yard—*nor a yard*, for cotton grew clear up to the door. But I have everything here! Here I will sing in the choir. You'll be able to spot in that choir those of us who suffered in the world. We'll be the ones who sing the loudest—and the most joyously!"

I like that point of view. For those who are suffering, death can mean the end of suffering and pain. It opens the way to joy and happiness. The death of a believer marks the advent of the greatest peace he or she has ever known.

The Way to "Professional" Fulfillment

Betty Pessaro told of her grandmother from England who was dying from cancer. Her grandfather had been an avid gardener. Betty's aunt and mother were sitting up at night watching over Betty's grandmother during those last days. One night they heard a knock at the door, but when they looked, no one was there. It happened a second and third time. The following morning when Betty's grandmother awoke, she said that she had spent the night in a garden so beautiful she could not even start to describe it. After her death, the family took comfort in the thought that her husband was maintaining that garden in heaven in anticipation of her arrival there, since he had enjoyed gardening so while here on earth.

If you love building, then materials, plans and creative thinking await you. If you love farming, then you can count on crops with no bugs, weeds, pesticides or droughts. I am sure rose growers will be busy, musicians will be happily working overtime. Nurses and doctors will undoubtedly have new professions.

Sharon Owens wrote to me from Lakewood, Colorado: "Last night I dreamed of my deceased dad. I asked, 'What are you doing up there?' He told me, 'We are preparing a place to your liking before the Lord comes to get you.' He looked to be in perfect health and told me, 'I have been doing a lot of welding, helping prepare the city.'"

Jesus was a carpenter. Is it so unlikely that He would work with His hands in heaven as He did on earth?

Being Safely Out of the Reach of Satan

I stand in the choir each Sunday morning at church beside a young lady named Jennifer who was thirteen when her daddy, Wellington Rose, died. He was an employee of Southern Railway and suffered a fatal heart attack.

Jennifer's mother told me later: "I stayed home with Jennifer while the pastor rushed my husband to the hospital. When Pastor Lowell pulled out of the driveway, I knelt and prayed. I felt a sudden burst of joy. I knew all was well."

The pastor later told her: "Driving Beltway 495, I prayed for Wellington, who was unconscious in the seat beside me. Then I fell quiet thinking about the joy of Easter near us on the calendar. Suddenly I heard Wellington say, 'Father, I'm Your son,' then, 'Jesus, I've been wanting to see You.' He waved his hand in greeting, then slumped against me, dead. We were just a few minutes from the hospital when it happened. There was an unexplainable, awesome power around us for about three seconds. It was not eerie, just strong and undeniable. It was like a tornado bottled up inside that car! Then it was gone. The doctor pronounced him dead upon arrival.

"Driving home I turned on the radio to hear Billy Graham preaching, telling how when Jesus came to earth angels accompanied Him through the 'principality zone of evil.' When Jesus died and returned to heaven, angels escorted Him back again through the atmosphere where Satan and his angels (the one-third cast out of heaven with him) reside. When a person dies, Satan will make a last attack on a soul that he is going to lose. At that moment God sends divine angelic forces to bring that person safely through that last attempt against his soul. He had brought Wellington in victoriously. I could almost see the reception committee."

As we will discuss later, Bible scholars surmise there are three heavens: one, the atmosphere of our earth; two, space or the expanse of the universe, which is occupied by the stars; and three, the heaven of heavens, God's eternal throne, outside of the time of our universe. It is the second of these that is considered to be the dwelling place of Satan, the "principality zone." The book of Jude (verse 9) tells how Michael the archangel contended with the devil over Moses' body when he died, saying, "The Lord rebuke you." Michael defeated Satan and ascended through this same zone.

Entering the Place of Eternal Joy

When I was about eleven, my father pastored two small churches in Rosedale and Clinton, Indiana. It was Easter Sunday and on the way home, sitting in the backseat of the car with my smaller brothers, I said, "I don't want to go to heaven."

My dad almost wrecked the car. Turning around he said, "The pastor's daughter doesn't want to go to heaven? You should not even talk like that in front of your little brothers."

I thought heaven was wall-to-wall church, and I had been born in church. We had revival meetings that lasted six to nine weeks, with not even Monday night or Saturday night off. Those were the days when pastors kept the visiting evangelists in their homes. When we had visiting preachers they used my bedroom, and I slept on the couch or on a daybed in my brother's room. I kept a diary, and one year I slept in my bed only 67 nights. I had been overexposed to heavenly topics.

Another reason I did not want to die and go to heaven was that one church I had attended seemed to think you had to wait until you got to heaven to have any pleasure. This concept did not appeal to me at all. I thought heaven was pale-faced people sitting on damp clouds playing harps. And judging from the Christmas cards we got, angels seemed to be meek robed things with soft hands and curls—or else fat, naked, dimpled babies playing little sequined harps.

It was not until my own death experience that I realized my perception of heaven's residents and the joy there was wrong. The angel who walked with me toward those gates of pearl must have been seven feet tall with large capable hands. He could have been a bouncer or a bodyguard. People up there were having fun,

29

building, working, getting on with real living. I arrived in the countryside (I am, after all, a country person) but could see the awesome city with a golden boulevard down the center, a sort of main street. That city, the capital of the planet of paradise, was beautiful and appealing to me and I longed to explore it.

Which brings us to the next point.

Unimaginable Travel and Exploration

As I walked toward those gates with my guardian angel at my side, I realized we could travel just by desire or wishing. Just as in our memories we can "travel" back to another time and place simply by wanting to, so we traveled at will but did so physically.

If the earth is but a footstool in God's immense house, then when we are with Him we will probably have travel access to the rest of the starry expanse as well. We will sweep through the universe as the Creator's children, exploring crowded nebulae, packed with orbs as thickly as the ocean beach is with sand.

Are these numberless worlds only lights in the firmament to illumine our little world at night? They have probably been prepared for habitation in God's eternal future, places for the development and expansion of redeemed humanity.

Perhaps this will start during our millennial reign with Jesus. Revelation tells us that His servants "shall serve Him" (22:3) and "shall reign forever and ever" (22:5) in the heavenly city, the headquarters of a vast universe.

I have heard people ask how we could travel through space without freezing to death. A country preacher I know put it in these fanciful terms: "Elijah was transported bodily to heaven, and he didn't turn to a block of ice on the way up. No, the Lord took care of that! He sent along a chariot of fire to keep Elijah warm all the way from here to glory. You're thinking furthermore that as Elijah rode that chariot of fire he could have been burned. No, God took care of that, too. He sent along a whirlwind to air-condition Elijah's chariot and keep him cool on his trip up yonder" (see 2 Kings 2:11).

The concept of travel in heaven has been described by a number of people who have been revived after a death experience. Travel is as quick as thought. I found that by simply thinking of a place I could be there instantaneously.

This possibility of instant time travel is beginning to sound less and less fantastic to scientists. *Time* magazine ran an article in January 1989 describing "of all the strange ideas in physics, perhaps the strangest." It is known as the wormhole, and acts as a sort of time machine or tunnel that might be "narrower than an atom" and "vanish the instant it formed."

It would not seem at all unlikely to me that scientists could begin to prove some of the stories told about death and the heavens. I believe that a great deal of time in heaven will be spent exploring the universe and studying laws of science.

The Greatest Communications Network Imaginable

In Livingston, Montana, I met Andy Lundgren. At age five he was given interesting insight into the possibility of a great communication network. He had had a brief brush with death and told me, "I went to a beautiful country. My grandma and grandpa met me there and introduced themselves. Since they had died before I was born, I wouldn't have known them. They showed me their beautiful house. One room had three king-sized beds and there were three or more big tables. The dinner was very good. Then they took me next door and showed me the house where my mother, dad and I would be moving into. My room was on the top floor where I could see the treetops, a pond and a stream. In my room I had *two* television sets.

"Mostly while I was there I played outdoors with an angel. We played tag and hide-and-seek. He would disappear and then appear and laugh. The angel showed me a place close to God's

31

throne; then I woke up. Now I know what to expect when I go there."

The parents rejoiced at this report, by the way, because they had been deeply concerned about whether or not Andy's grandfather had received Jesus and eternal life before he died. They were comforted by their son's unsolicited report.

My first reaction was, "That's just like a kid to want not one, but two TV sets!" Then I received a letter from Len LeSourd that offered some insight on the little boy's vision and the communications network in heaven. He wrote: "Since not many of us have had the privilege like you to have had a glimpse into the next world, we have to use our imaginations somewhat to picture it. My imagination runs wild whenever I dwell on the subject. I see an incredible communications network that would make the biggest and greatest computer we have in our world today look like a child's toy."

That is particularly relevant in relation to a learning system I believe is in operation for infants and young children who arrive in heaven not having been instructed concerning Jesus' birth, death and resurrection. If "there is nothing new under the sun" (Ecclesiastes 1:9), God merely renews and reviews for each new generation. One author suggests that dramas are presented in great theaters, so people can review the lives of Jesus, the martyrs, their ancestors and their loved ones.

Ann Sandberg in *Seeing the Invisible* states that while "God is concerned with a great deal more than how many He can get into heaven, He is interested in numbers, for we read that in heaven the angels . . . rejoice over every additional sinner whose repentance they register" (see Luke 15:10).

Are these events that cause rejoicing recorded on some sort of "computer" for review into eternity?

It seems conceivable that God might also have assigned some angels to "computers" that make entries of spiritual development. We are told that "they that feared the LORD spake often one to another: and the LORD hearkened, and heard it, and a book of remembrance was written before him for them that . . . thought upon his name" (Malachi 3:16, KJV). Could it be that records are kept of the individual Christian's progress? Is the Potter observing the vessel take shape and keeping a computerized record the way a parent on earth would compile a scrapbook or photo album?

Perfect Justice

This could seem hard to believe in the face of so many trials that are hard to understand. I have a picture that was sent to me by a young mother in Loveland, Colorado. She had put her eighteen-month-old baby into her car seat and begun a short drive.

Suddenly, at an intersection she felt a sickening jolt. A man out on bond for drunk driving had rented a truck and, influenced by alcohol, had run the light. That mother picked herself up from the ditch and, to her horror, saw that the whole backseat of her car was gone. The baby was in the middle of the highway, badly injured. The little girl is now two years old. She just lies in her bed, eyes open, seemingly unconscious.

How can we comprehend something as unfair as this? Or other injustices we hear of, such as honest people being cheated, good people being slandered, kind people being abused?

How can we comprehend other heartbreaking tragedies such as the one a missionary friend of ours suffered? He backed out of his driveway one morning not knowing that one of his children was playing behind the wheels of the car. The child was killed. Their other living child is severely mentally disabled.

These families and many others who face the trauma of pain and heartache need our prayers and support. And they need to be reminded of the hope of heaven.

While there may be inequality and injustice in this life, there is only righteousness in heaven. Every action will be "proclaimed upon the housetops" (Luke 12:3) and that means that those who were wronged or falsely accused will be vindicated. Everyone who has been hurt by the selfishness or rejection of others will revel in the love of Jesus. All wrongs will be righted. That young mother will find her daughter healthy and strong. The missionary and his wife will enjoy eternity with their fully restored children.

Looking back to my teens I recall that when the services at church would drag and people's attention seemed to wander, my father would call on another girl my age, Knoxie Crabtree (now Frost), and me to sing a duet. She played her guitar and I my accordion. We are probably much too "mature" to do this now, but then, young, in love with two men in the congregation and of free spirit, we would sing joyously.

One of the songs we sang was called "I Would Not Miss It, Would You?" and it spoke of Jesus' return. One of the promises of His coming was that "wrongs are made right and forgiveness is sought."

Yes, there is a place where scores are settled and the books are balanced. But not here. After death we will find the justice we are seeking.

The Replacement of Fear with Love

A newspaper interview told the story of Augustine Chiedozie of Lagos, Nigeria. Augustine had died in a hospital in Aba on August 31, 1985. He had just finished a meal and appeared to have suffocated. He was dead for twelve hours.

Meanwhile, a doctor was reading the Bible before retiring for the evening and came across John 11:4: "This sickness is not unto death, but for the glory of God." He went to the hospital after dreaming that Augustine had recovered—and found that

Death: A Point of View

he had. The newspaper account showed a picture of the six nurses who had attended his body and prepared him for burial.

When Augustine came back, he told them that the word *love* means "God." He arrived at this conclusion standing at the tail end of a long queue above a carpet of clouds: "I stood in line. A fierce-looking angel was manning a very narrow gate. There was an expansive table on which lay a massive book. I saw my name and four outstanding charges against me. Beside the book was a golden goblet of blood and a brush with a golden handle. The angel received a word from headquarters and stroked the blood across the charges four times.

"Suddenly the glory and splendor of music broke across the air waves and the trees and birds swayed to the rhythm of the joyous anthem."

Augustine was told to come back and report what he saw. He was also told to serve humanity with love and without charge.

What should our point of view be about death? Perhaps one in which we trust Jesus completely, with no room for doubt or fear.

Looking Forward to that Better Country

Last evening Carl and I sat on the upstairs sundeck of our little house here in Florida, feet propped up on the rail around the porch up among the treetops. We were laughing so loudly, my neighbor Robin looked our way from her car window to see what was happening over here. Let's have some fun at our own expense. This is what brought on the raucous laughter.

Carl said that when he dies he wants inscribed on the tombstone the words God said to Moses, "My presence shall go with thee and I will give thee *rest*." Then, to add some zest to the funeral, he suggested asking Lowell Lundstrom to sing his funny song, "U-Haul." The gist of the song is that you never see a hearse with a U-Haul trailer behind it. You can't take it with you!

I told Carl to save money and not buy a coffin. "Bury me in my 'green machine,'" I said. That is the nifty 1962 MGA convertible I have driven so long. We both laughed at this since all our children want it when I go. Then, since I was writing this book about the afterlife, he could not resist saying, "Shall we bury the car nose-down to give you a headstart?"

I asked Carl to tell God not to have any telephones for me up there. I would enjoy being buried beneath a palm tree, or being dumped into the ocean. I love the beach. Then I told him not to spend a lot of money on a tombstone. Take a piece of wood and with a purple crayon write, "I made it!" We laughed and the conversation got sillier.

We discussed our mothers-in-law. His mother, Rose Malz, was a big-framed German woman. My mother, Fern Burns Perkins, was a small-framed Scottish/English blend. They are both in heaven.

We visualized the two of them, sewing, sitting at a small, white, wrought-iron table on a lovely balcony with flowers below (they both liked flowers) looking down at the serenity of the flowing river while discussing us, Carl and Betty, their children.

We could just hear Mrs. Malz: "Betty was lucky to get Carl. He could have done better." She sips her tea. "Betty was never missionary material. I know a hundred women who would have adjusted better to him."

To which my little mother retorts, "Poor baby. Betty is having a hard time adjusting. Carl is a man of strong preference. You can always tell a German, but you can't tell him much!"

They sip on rather than argue in heaven.

My first husband, John, is living in a waterfront home. Of this I am sure. He loved to water ski.

Carl and I could see John chatting with Carl's first wife, Wanda, sitting on another balcony farther down the river. They must have heard our mothers-in-law. The two of them really know us both and were laughing their heads off saying, "They deserve each other."

Of course, that was all made up in our imaginations, but it underscored for us the fact that death is not a fearful subject. It is not something we discuss in reverent whispers, as if we were unsure of our destination or unclear about what we will find on the other side.

Do you fear death? I would like to share with you an old Gospel song passed down many generations. I first heard it years ago when my grandparents sang it at Lake Placid, Indiana, Camp Meeting U.S.A. My mother had scribbled the words on some notebook paper before she died, and I have taken them with me on my many moves—from North Dakota to Florida to Texas back to the Dakotas and now back to Florida again.

I took the paper out of my piano bench early this morning, played and sang it again. It has a lullaby rhythm and soothing words. If you have any fear left about death, perhaps it will minister to you as it has to so many others. I can almost hear Mom Burns, my grandma, humming it now:

> A country where no storm cloud shadows deepen,
>   Unending day, where night shall never be;
> A land removed from sickness, pain and sorrow
>   Oh, this is just what heaven means to me.
>
> A place where there are no misunderstandings,
>   Where from all enmity and strife we're free;
> No unkind words to wound the heart are spoken,
>   Oh, this is just what heaven means to me.
>
> Where we shall see at last the face of Jesus,
>   Before whose image other loves all flee;
> And when they crown Him Lord of all I'll be there,
>   Oh, this is just what heaven means to me.

Chorus:
What will it be when we get over yonder
  And join that throng upon the glassy sea?
We'll meet our loved ones and crown Christ forever,
  Yes, this is just what heaven means to me.

It takes faith to believe that death is nothing to fear. It takes faith to get to that ultimate place of peace—heaven. The Bible tells us that without faith it is impossible to please God (see Hebrews 11:6). But if we do believe, then our anticipation can be like an unseen hand that takes hold of us and leads us to that better country, through the doorway we call death.

3

Questions about Life in Heaven

One day not long ago I felt panicked that time was getting short to complete this book to meet my publishing deadline. Yet my whole day was cut up like a tossed salad and my computer was constipated; nothing wanted to flow out! The phone rang. The doorbell rang and rang.

I finally put a red plastic sign on the doorknob: *Do not disturb. I am writing.* I heard a knock. Looking up I saw a woman peeping through the window watching me. She called out, "Does this mean me?"

Before I could catch myself I retorted, "Only if you can read." Then, feeling guilty for being rude, I opened the door and lost an hour of time that I had wanted to spend working.

As soon as she left I skated toward the bookshelf to grab more paper and reached for a large box containing letters to me from people in foreign lands. I almost concluded they would lie there for the next two weeks, but then I picked up one or two and began to review the contents—the rejoicing and reports of miraculous heavenly thoughts. You read some of them in the last chapter.

As I read more of those letters from all parts of the world from people looking for Jesus to come back I realized suddenly how day-to-day worries were causing me to lose sight of the blessed hope: "Many shall come from the east and west, and shall sit down with Abraham, and Isaac, and Jacob, in the kingdom of heaven" (Matthew 8:11, KJV). That is the important thing, joining other believers in the heavenly Kingdom in order to worship God.

Life in Heaven

The questions about heaven asked in those letters are basically the same questions people ask about life. Suppose a couple contemplates a move to California or back home to Minnesota. Generally they sit down and concern themselves with six things:

1. Where will we live?
2. What will we eat?
3. What will we wear?
4. What about transportation?
5. What kind of work will we do?
6. What about the children?

Here is the way I would answer those questions—and others—as they relate to heaven.

Where Will We Live?

The Bible says that in heaven we will live forever in mansions that Jesus prepares (see John 11:26; 14:2). We will live near Him, close to His place.

Rebecca Springer told me of a vision she was given of heaven. She believes that many have a mountain home, a city home, a place by the river or, for the farmer, a country home.

My cousin Pam's husband, David, said he would rather not go if he cannot go fishing. My Uncle Bud is there now and I am convinced he has a boat and is enjoying dinners of fresh-caught fish. The word *river* is mentioned two hundred times in the Bible. I have not counted how many times the words *sea, stream* and *ocean* are recorded, but it seems as though they are important in God's scheme of things and will be plentiful.

What Will We Eat?

Probably some fish, quail, fowl, manna, angel's food (whatever they eat), cakes, corn and the bread of heaven (see Psalm 78:24–28; 105:40). I believe that whatever God provided for the people of Israel in the journey through the wilderness He will provide in heaven—and better. God puts touches of heaven on earth: "Every good thing bestowed and every perfect gift is from above, coming down from the Father of lights" (James 1:17).

Two people who have died and returned to life wrote me of eating juicy pears from the Tree of Life, which bears twelve kinds of fruit (see Revelation 22:2). Much is said about trees in the Bible. The same verse in Revelation talks about the leaves of the trees being used for the healing of the nations. I believe we will find vegetation and many fresh vegetables. We will have the ultimate connoisseur's taste and access to the satisfaction of that taste!

To a child heaven would be candy. Italians might want lasagna. Greeks might prefer fêta cheese and seafood. Babies will want milk. Old folks might not be able to eat steak here, but I feel sure their teeth can tolerate it there, if there is meat.

In Canaan the land was flowing with milk and honey. The God who made Eden and so many fine foods here on earth will not shortchange us there.

A little fellow asked me a strange question. He wondered if there would be toilets there. My Aunt Pearl and I are nearly the same age. Mother's youngest sister is more like the sister I never had. As kids at our grandparents' country house in Indiana we used to sit in the outdoor toilet at night, gaze at the stars, and wish we could stay long enough on a trip to the outhouse so we would not have to return ever again and waste our time. We preferred to spend our time playing. But it never worked that way.

I suppose in heaven there is nothing wasted and, therefore, no waste material. Perhaps the little fellow was not so far off in asking that question. I guess God does not have to answer all our questions now. Some will have to wait. Deity reserves some crown rights!

What Will We Wear?

The owner of a local boutique saw me in the dressing room of her shop and asked me what they wear in heaven. There are many Scriptures that speak of robes. Oden Hetrick said he saw three garments: People were clothed in humility, righteousness and garments of praise, three distinct layers.

He said that the garment of humility looked like a soft undergarment. The next layer, the robe of righteousness, was very shiny. The top layer, the garment of praise, was a sleeveless coat or vest that fell below the knee. It was beautiful and ornate, covered with precious stones.

He said he remembered most people as being barefoot. The children of Israel in the wilderness wore the same shoes for forty years, and those shoes did not wear out on their walk to Canaan. I suppose God could provide holy soles to last forever if He so desired.

Robert Mosley tells the story about a Communist orator who was holding forth in London's Trafalgar Square expounding upon the advantages of Communism. Alongside him, standing on another soapbox, was an evangelist telling of the glories of Jesus' saving grace and heaven.

An unshaven, unkempt derelict of a man was standing between the two soapboxes in the forefront of the crowd. The Communist spotted him, pointed his finger and shouted, "Ladies and gentlemen, Communism can put a new suit on that man."

The evangelist responded by saying, "Ladies and gentlemen, God can put a new man in that suit."

Bobbie Morrison introduced me to her friend Norman Milley. In June 1976 he suffered a massive heart attack while living in Norwood, Massachusetts. They called his family together, and he lingered in a coma for eight days.

During this time he was launched into the glory of God in another world. He says it is impossible to describe it in words. He met an angel who informed him that Jesus' blood had cleansed him from all sin (see 1 John 1:7). He walked along the River of Life, which flowed from under the city of God. Trees were lining the crystal flow. Another angel appeared to him, held out a gloriously white robe and began to help him put it on.

He cried out, "Oh, please let me put it on!"

The angel said, "First we must remove the robe that you now have on, for 'this corruptible must put on incorruption, and this mortal must put on immortality'" (see 1 Corinthians 15:53, KJV).

When Norman came to, the doctor was taking his blood pressure and he was crying out, "I want to put it on! I want to go. I want to take off this robe and put on the new one." They said he was tearing at his hospital gown, trying to replace it with an unseen garment.

He explained to the doctor what had happened to him, where he had been and what he had seen. In a matter of hours he was out of intensive care and improving remarkably. He has already lived ten extra years, and has not forgotten the wonder of that new robe.

What about Transportation?

Isaiah speaks of seeing the King in His beauty and walking with God high in salvation along the climes of bliss. I love walking and this is all right with me, but the Scriptures also speak of many chariots of God up there. I have the written accounts of three who have died and who talk about chariots.

The vast size of heaven and the immense city will require good transportation, though we have forever to see it all. Since there is no hurry, chariots are furnished perhaps more for enjoyment than speed.

I estimate that they travel at least at the speed of sound and are propelled by the power of God: no motors, no fuel. The vehicles can travel over land, river or sky. During my own death experience, I found walking to be effortless uphill and down. It is more like a sensation of movement, like *being* more than *going*. And, as I mentioned in the last chapter, travel can also be as quick as thought.

It sounds exciting to me. The Scriptures bear out the fact that "in Thy presence is fulness of joy; in Thy right hand there are pleasures forever" (Psalm 16:11).

There is an unsmiling man in my neighborhood who would be uncomfortable there. He teaches the eleventh commandment: "Thou shalt have no fun on earth." Let me be clear: I believe in the Bible basics. And a foundational principle is that heaven is a blissful Kingdom of great joy and—forgive the child's expression—fun.

What Kind of Work Will We Do?

We will be set free from unrest. There will be no need to prove anything to anyone. We will no longer be prisoners of impressions or competition. But we will need employment for ultimate fulfillment, to make life most real to every individual personality.

My mother loved color and flowers and she loved to sew. I think she is making drapes for my mansion and helping with the color schemes and interior decoration for the houses of my four brothers and their wives before we arrive.

She also loved to visit us and rearrange our furniture. We used to get aggravated at her for doing this, but we let her. Then we changed things back after she left. God love her, I would never wish her back to suffer cancer again, but if I had it to do over, I would accommodate her and others more.

I think Aunt Lillian is painting. She was a gifted artist here. My two grandfathers, Dad Perky and Dad Burns, and my first father-in-law, Oscar Upchurch, were contractors, carpenters, builders, roofers. They helped us build family homes and know what we like.

I still have the last hammer that my Uncle Leon Rogers worked with before he died. It seems likely that God has upgraded his tools for heaven's kitchen cabinet patterns.

I laugh now remembering Dad Burns' eightieth birthday. He finished putting a roof on a house, came home at noon to eat his birthday cake with us grandchildren and said, "I retire." He was an energetic man and I am sure is gainfully employed hammering and nailing up there.

My friend Lawrence Douglas is only 82 and still tends his tangerine groves and rides his Appaloosa. He will find plenty to do when he gets to heaven in all the fruit groves over on the hillside of glory.

Mom Perky, my paternal grandmama, loved to cook and give things away. She is undoubtedly helping plan the menu for the Marriage Supper of Jesus and His Bride, the Church. My two aunts are like her. Each Thanksgiving I get a couple of packages from Aunt Shirley and Aunt Elsie. They mail me sage from Mom Perky's herb garden in Indiana, from her old home place, to spice up my stuffing for the turkey.

As I have mentioned, my first husband, John, died at age 36 following open heart surgery. The doctor gave him the option of not having surgery and slowing down his lifestyle. John chose the surgery. He said he would rather enjoy a short life than be bored and live twice as long. He was an achiever and motivator, winning awards from his company for volume business and new promotional ideas. John was also an outdoors person. It was almost as though he lived twice as long in half the time, completing his assignments here early. Over there I imagine that he is teaching people to water ski on the River of Life.

Mom Burns was of a different breed. She never made a fuss about housekeeping. She loved us kids and picking berries and making jam. We could jump up and down on the beds, ransack her attic, pour out the button box onto the floor and leave it, climb the cherry tree, climb onto the cows' backs and bring pets into the living room. We never bothered or crowded her. I would bet she is rocking my baby brother up there until we all arrive.

Bottom line, I believe we will enjoy doing there whatever we enjoy doing here. But our work will not be toil. It will be joyful employment of all the powers of the soul.

So, if you enjoy agriculture, you will enjoy your visits to the plains, valleys, hills and mountains of splendor in paradise. If you are a teacher here, you may greatly relish instructing those who have just come from terrestrial shores to the eternal Kingdom. Those who are mechanics and engineers will find ample scope for expression there, helping the Lord prepare our mansions, employing the busy hands of millions of His saints in the most wonderful architecture of heaven.

We will look like ourselves and act like ourselves at our very best. Job said, remember, "And though . . . worms destroy this body, yet *in my flesh* shall I see God" (19:26, KJV, emphasis added).

Luke 24:39 tells us that Jesus' resurrected body was intact: "See My hands and My feet, that it is I Myself; touch Me and see, for a spirit does not have flesh and bones as you see that I have." Jesus talked and ate with the disciples. Yet in His resurrected body, Jesus could pass through closed doors, appear, disappear, transport Himself from place to place and finally ascend to heaven.

When Jesus returns for His Bride, we will be given our resurrected bodies. Thus, we, too, will have glorified physical bodies like His (see 1 Thessalonians 4:16–17). "When He appears, we shall be like Him, because we shall see Him just as He is" (1 John 3:2).

Further, we will be known as we are known here. Let me quote again Jesus' words: "And I say to you, that many shall come from east and west, and recline at table with Abraham, and Isaac, and Jacob, in the kingdom of heaven" (Matthew 8:11). In other words, they will not have lost their identities.

What about the Children?

The Bible speaks so much about children that that subject alone could fill an entire book. Children who die young are not unhappy being taken from us. There is no discontent or sorrow there, only supreme joy. No change of place or surroundings could make them happier, unless it would be to see their parents, brothers, sisters or friends arrive, too. When that happens, then their cup of happiness will be full indeed. Be sure to prepare to meet them.

I hope that those who have lost children can take comfort in the knowledge of how much Jesus loves them. "Let the children come to Me," He said. And I have always loved the words of the song "Jesus Loves Me," the first song we learn as babies: *Little ones to Him belong.*

One man saw angels in a vision leaving heaven, going to earth to get children when they were dying. A multitude of mothers and Sunday school teachers are there who are loving and teaching the little ones.

In her vision of heaven Rebecca Springer reports that she saw the young daughter of a friend arrive in heaven and heard the mother pray: "O God, she is such a shy child and we have no one there to meet her or care for her when she arrives."

Rebecca saw her nestled lovingly in the Master's arms. Then, as she was sitting comfortably in His lap, a remarkably fine white Angora kitten ran across the grass and sprang into her welcoming arms. It purred, rubbing its head under the child's chin, and then lay down and fell asleep in her lap.

The family had not been able to find the kitten since the child's death. Who but our loving Father would have thought of such a comfort for a little girl? She had been timid on earth, but as other children gathered around her, she had delightful freedom manifested in Jesus' presence.

An angel in Rebecca's vision told her: "We have watched over you and others from your infancy. As a child on earth is instructed by a parent about heaven, so we teach children here about earth."

Our Father never forgets us. He provides every pleasure and comfort for us all according to our individual needs.

Perhaps this is why children seem to arrive in the garden Paradise part of heaven instead of directly at the throne—so the change will not be too great for them. They progress happily to the suburbs of heaven to play among the flowers and along the streams. If you want to know what heaven is like, read the Genesis account of Eden. The Bible tells us that God planted that Garden. That was, perhaps, a transplanted garden from heaven.

Dr. W. B. McCafferty says that old age is the mark of sickness and death. On the other hand, "older people will become youthful and infants will grow slowly and surely in the nurture of the wholesome atmosphere of heaven." They cannot get sick or be injured. And there is no aging or death there, or drugs or perversion. Indeed, there can be no sin at all in the dwelling place of God!

If a day is as a thousand years with God, I think that the children will not be a lot older than they were when they were lost to us. Physically, as with our spiritual growth, God does not see me as I am, but as I am going to be. If you have lost a child, you can be sure He has an ultimate growing up for your baby. There is no incompleteness in heaven. You can be sure as well that your preemie is complete or that a miscarried child awaits you there or that aborted babies are alive and well. All of us will be in the springtime of our lives. The climate there is "forever spring"!

One born-again Catholic nun told me that she believes she will mother children over there whose mothers did not make it because of unbelief in Jesus. Some loving women—perhaps those who were barren or unmarried on earth—will care for those children there.

One near-death account I read recorded this conversation of child to mother: "It is better that I did not grow up down there in that world. I might have been a bad woman. God knew best." The parent later read Isaiah 57:1 (KJV): "The righteous is taken away from the evil to come." She felt it applied specifically to her child's situation, and it gave her comfort.

Marietta Davis claims she saw infants singing in a children's choir in her glimpse of heaven. They had lessons in music and singing and even formed bands. They were also instructed about the birth, life and death of Jesus. She said the children wore or carried beautiful flowers. In heaven's great worship Temple, they sat in small seats reserved for them, marked by a thousand golden chains set with diamonds and gems of rarest beauty.

I received this letter from a mother in Birch Run, Michigan:

In 1980 I lost two of my three little girls in a car accident along with their grandpa, gramma, and three cousins. My daughters were six and eight. I cried out to God, "I must know some way that they are in heaven for sure."

It was a difficult task to go to their school to clean out their little desks. In my eight-year-old's desk there was only one paper. She had drawn a picture of her and her younger sister holding hands going up into the air to heaven, with wings, into a beautiful, colorful sky. Immediately I had peace in my heart knowing where they were.

Unless you lose someone very dear to you, I don't think you really take so much interest in heaven. I can't hear enough now.

People rarely believe in miracles until they need one. I believe this is why God often shows us the way in life through the faith of a simple, believing child or an adult with a child's faith.

What about Contact with the Dead?

This brings up an important point. Some ask me if there is contact with those in heaven. Make no mistake about it: There is danger in trying to contact the dead. The Bible strictly prohibits it as an occult practice. Do not try it. Talk instead to God. Pour out your thoughts, worries and fears to Him and He will hear and help you, just as He helped this mother and countless others. He alone is our heavenly Comforter, Guide and Friend. Pray to the Father in the name of Jesus, His Son.

I should point out, however, that some, such as Sadhu Sundar Singh, believe that on rare occasions God allows us glimpses or impressions of our dead loved ones, perhaps in a dream or vision—such as some we have already seen.

I told in *Prayers That Are Answered* how I was pregnant with our second child when John died. April was born four months after her daddy's death.

At the hospital, when they brought her to me and laid her tiny little head on my arm, I wished John had lived long enough to see her just once, for a few minutes, even.

Suddenly in the doorway I caught a glimpse of white. Looking up, thinking a nurse was trying to get my attention, I saw John standing there. He flashed me a big, proud, boyish grin and was gone.

I do not know why God allowed me that experience. But I do know that I did not then, and would not now, seek it. If He chose to give me comfort in that manner I can only accept it with a grateful heart.

. . . And Other Questions

Perhaps you have other questions.

I have often wondered, for instance, if we will have knowledge in heaven of our loved ones who will not be joining us there. Will we miss those friends and relatives who choose to live their lives without believing in Jesus and, thus, will spend eternity without Him?

Revelation 21:4 says, "He shall wipe away every tear." Our hearts will be full of the emotions of praise with no thought of weeping about anything. Our faculties and dispositions to sorrow or sadness will be gone, and we will see things as God sees them.

This says to me that people in heaven know what is happening here on earth, but they are not depressed by sad events. They are in eternal bliss, happy with God's all-wise planning.

Hebrews 12:1, referring to prophets and martyrs and the believers who have gone on before us, says: "Wherefore seeing we [the living] also are compassed about with so great a cloud of witnesses . . . let us run with patience the race that is set before us" (KJV).

In this regard, Roberts Lairdon said he saw a sports stadium, something like football bleachers, with many hosts of people in the stands facing the outer perimeter of heaven and looking down upon earth. They were cheering, standing, waving banners and flags, and rooting for us here while we witness, sing and work for the Lord. They knelt to pray for us, he said, while some here were preaching and witnessing to unbelievers.

Have you ever wondered what language we will speak in heaven? No matter what language we speak on earth, I am sure we will fully understand each other there. Again, 1 John 3:2 says: "When He appears, we shall be like Him, because we shall see Him just as He is." He hears all the voices of the earth that are petitioning Him at the same time and is not confused at all. I personally feel that we will comprehend all the languages. We will be multilingual and speak and communicate with people of all nations and tongues. Many scholars suggest that we will speak the original language of Eden, the language that Adam and Eve spoke when they walked and talked with God. Do you remember that before the Tower of Babel, the world spoke one universal language? God confused their tongues because of their greed, competition and pride. There will be none of that in heaven.

Will animals be in heaven?

I heard from one person who died who saw little children laughing, running hither and yon catching tiny birds in their hands, singing and playing with animals. Many have reported seeing open countryside with plenty of space for animals to explore.

The Bible mentions a lot of animals. In the Millennium, the lion will lie down with the lamb. Much is written about horses and eagles. In Revelation 19:17 birds are told to come. And Acts 11:5–10 describes Peter's vision in which a great sheet is lowered from heaven containing four-footed animals, wild beasts, crawling creatures and birds.

I think that whatever animals are there will be harmless and will have glorified personalities just as we will. The wolf and the lamb, for instance, shall feed together and none will be hurt.

Will the soul of a pet survive the gates of death? God created animals in the Garden for Adam's pleasure and can resurrect them if He so desires. He makes the rules. It is impossible to say whether or not your animals will be there but of this I am sure: Nothing is impossible with God. If His plan for our happiness includes the survival of our pets, then they will most assuredly be there.

In fact, Rebecca Springer also saw children in her vision who were playing in a grassy meadow, rolling and tumbling over a big dog with great freedom. As she approached, the dog broke away from them and came bounding to meet her, crouching and fawning at her feet in welcome. It was her dear Sport, their family dog. She hugged his neck, burying her face in his silken fur. The dog understood every word she spoke. And his fur! He splashed in the river every day, and it left a mark on his coat.

One of the sweetest proofs of our Father's loving care for us is that it seems we will find in heaven the small things that gave us great happiness below.

I am also asked many questions about marriage in heaven. We will know no sorrow there, nor is there any unfulfilled desire that cannot be fully met in heaven. Jesus said that there is no marriage in heaven—"in the resurrection they neither marry, nor are given in marriage" (Matthew 22:30)—but if a godly companion is your deep desire I believe you will be satisfied there. Millions of meaningful relationships will be possible. There will definitely be no differences in faith, no unequal yoking. It is completely possible that there will be personal, intimate relationships in heaven lasting forever—but with no reproduction.

God is love, and He is the One who initiated the idea of mates for Adam and Eve. They were joined in marriage in order to populate the earth. We are not sure how full the earth would have become had Adam and Eve not sinned and caused death to enter the picture, nor how they would have been transported to heaven. We do know, however, that there is no death in heaven and no need for repopulation to replace lost humanity. If a woman is pregnant when she dies or when Jesus comes, she will have the first painless childbirth—for she and her child will arrive in a place where there is no suffering.

Some marriages here are made in heaven. It does not seem likely to me that God will break up a good relationship. If you have a loving relationship with a spouse or sweetheart it will remain in heaven—even be enhanced! There is no reason to believe it will be diminished; indeed, this reunion of sweethearts may be one of heaven's chief joys.

Some marriage companionships have lasted more than half a century and could go on throughout the ages. Why not? The Bible says, "What therefore God has joined together, let no man separate" (Matthew 19:6). Some people rush into marriages that were not intended to be in the first place. In heaven God's perfect will shall be done. In heaven it will be as it should have been on earth. I believe God knows a person somewhere made just for you. If you do not find him or her here, perhaps there. If you are happily joined in union with another, your love and oneness will be far sweeter there than it ever was here.

Suppose you have been widowed three times on earth. Which husband or wife will you prefer in heaven? It is questions like these that make the idea "one per customer" seem like good advice! Perhaps we can think about it this way. In heaven our first love will be Jesus. There is no jealousy or competition there, only unity and harmony. You may well prefer relatives and old friends to new acquaintances, but, in general, everyone will have perfect love for everyone else.

I am often asked about wayward children and heaven. Some parents seem to do everything right and yet their kids go wrong. I think in this situation we must stand on the Word: "For I know whom I have believed, and am persuaded that he is able to keep that which I have committed unto him against that day" (2 Timothy 1:12, KJV).

The prophet Jeremiah said,

> Thus says the LORD, "A voice is heard in Ramah, lamentation and bitter weeping. Rachel is weeping for her children . . . because they are no more. . . . Restrain your voice from weeping, and your eyes from tears; for your work shall be rewarded." declares the LORD, "and they shall return from the land of the enemy. And there is hope for your future . . . and your children shall return to their own territory."
>
> Jeremiah 31:15–17

The Bible also tells us, "Train up a child in the way he should go: and when he is old, he will not depart from it" (Proverbs 22:6, KJV). Or, as my dad used to tell us, "Do your best and the Lord will make up the difference."

These Scriptures can help sustain us as we pray for our children to turn their lives over to the Lord, but how do we pray when a young person—or adult—has already died or chooses to end his life by suicide?

When Carl pastored a church in Texas, we received a call to come and support a couple whose seventeen-year-old son had hanged himself with his belt. I talked with a Christian medical doctor hoping to find help for them.

He said he believed that if a child has been taught of Jesus, and if someone is currently praying for him, the child will be given one last chance either to receive or reject God at the end.

This physician believes that a person's mind continues to function for about 56 seconds after death occurs; a person can do a lot of praying in that time.

A man called me to report, for instance, that he had had cardiac arrest and had cried out, "Jesus, save me!" He did not think he would live and wanted to take a leap of faith, a last plea that God would consider saving him and letting him into His heaven.

He was given a second chance at life and said he remembered well the last sermon he heard before the heart attack. The minister's text was: "It is time to seek the Lord" (Hosea 10:12). Recalling the Scripture in that sermon brought that man to his soul's knees and his heart offered a "rescue prayer" at the last moment.

We can hope that the searching hearts of these young people who have ended their lives reached out to the love of Jesus as well. We must always cling to God's mercy. There is always hope. Difficult questions like this one about death are where prayer, faith and trust take hold.

When answers seem hard to find, remember that without Christ something is always wanting. When we are young we have grand enterprises, but no experience. When we are old we have the experience, but then the power and energy to carry out our schemes are gone. In heaven we will have both! "Happy is he that hath the God of Jacob for his help, whose hope is in the LORD his God" (Psalm 146:5, KJV).

There is no doubt we have many questions about heaven that will have to wait for answers until we arrive there. God does not have to explain everything to us here. As we have noted, Deity reserves some crown rights. Wait patiently for Him. Time is just nature's way of keeping everything from happening all at once. God's timing and His answers are always perfect.

4

Where Is Heaven?

My favorite response to the question "Where is heaven?" is a line from an old hymn: "Where Jesus is, 'tis heaven there!" Another song says that "He is as close as the mention of His name."

Heaven is not so far away that God cannot hear us when we pray. He is accessible to everyone through prayer. This does not mean, however, that heaven is only an ethereal sort of spiritual place, unapproachable in a physical sense. It is a very real place occupied by very real inhabitants. Jesus said He will come back and take us there (see John 14:1–4).

Interesting Sights in Space

Part of the heavenlies is visible, for the Bible tells us that in the last days there will be signs in the heavens (probably the second heaven we identified earlier) and in the earth (within earth's atmosphere—the first heaven). Perhaps some of these signs are becoming evident as we learn more about our universe as it relates to heaven.

Astronomers tell us, for instance, that there is a huge opening or cavity in the constellation of Orion—a nebula—that is perhaps 139 trillion miles in diameter. (The diameter of the earth's orbit around the sun is about 186 million miles.) Said one telescopic observer from the Mt. Lowe Observatory in New Mexico:

> But surpassing the immensity of its size is its exquisite beauty and the luminous colors that are unlike any on earth. The opening and interior are so stupendous that our entire solar system would be lost therein. . . . The depth reveals rivers and masses of shining glass, irregular pillars, columns of stalactites and stalagmites from the mighty floor. The appearance is like that of light shining and glowing behind clear walls of ivory and pearl, studded with millions of diamonds like shining stars.

Is this perhaps a glimpse of a heavenly realm? There must be a reason why all this splendor is lavished on this one spot in the heavens. At any rate, it is no wonder that many scientists claim to feel a connection with the Almighty while scanning this great outburst of grandeur.

I find it interesting to hear about unusual sightings reported by pilots in the earth's atmosphere and by astronauts zipping through space. My favorite phenomenal sighting was reported by Dr. Kurt Bauer, a German astrophysicist. He claims to have viewed photographs taken by a Soviet space probe that seem to resemble heaven. "The pictures are remarkable in their similarity to what people have seen during near-death experiences," he says.

I have not seen these photographs, and can in no way verify their authenticity, but apparently darkness gives way to a rainbow-colored tunnel of light that opens to "an unearthly green and yellow landscape" of an area that looks like "a great walled city."

Bauer claims that hundreds of these pictures were beamed back to earth. Russian officials, apparently, did not confirm or deny the story. They did state that Bauer worked with Soviet scientists and would have had access to any such photographs "if they do exist."

Other amazing stories have popped up in the media purporting to relate to heaven and its place in space. The *Houston Chronicle*, for instance, reported in January 1986 that six Soviet cosmonauts claimed to have seen a band of glowing angels. "What we saw," they said, "were seven giant figures in the form of humans, but with wings and mistlike halos, as in the classic depiction of angels." Angels are the messengers of God, traveling from the throne room to the earth to carry out their missions. Could they have been glimpsed en route? There is really no way to tell.

The Clarifying Scriptures

Scripture, on the other hand, does give us some specifics to ponder about God's creation. Consider with me this interesting insight on the location of heaven. Isaiah 14:13 tells us that heaven is "above the stars of God" and "in the recesses of the north." Since stars encircle the earth, "north" could be considered "up" from every part of the globe. Thus, wherever a believer is when he dies, it seems his spirit would go "up."

When Paul spoke of being "caught up into the third heaven" (see 2 Corinthians 12:2) he not only indicated direction, but gave us the understanding that there are first and second heavens as well. These all were completed in the six days of creation (see Genesis 2:1), made by God's mighty power for His wonderful purposes.

The first heaven, as we have noted, is the atmosphere around us, the air we breathe, the place where birds and airplanes fly, where clouds are formed and earth's gravity takes effect. Matthew 24:30–31 tells us that at the Second Coming of Christ, the sign of the Son of Man will appear in the sky, visible to those on earth, and then Jesus will come "on the clouds of the sky with power and great glory. And He will send forth His angels with a great trumpet and they will gather together His elect from the four winds, from one end of the sky to the other."

The second heaven is the starry space of the firmament above us, where the moon, the stars and the galaxies revolve. With powerful telescopes, scientists are able to see many quintillion miles into space.

These first two realms are readily visible, though we see only glimpses of the spiritual encounters taking place in them. I mentioned that many Bible scholars feel that the second heaven is where Satan and the angels who rebelled with him were sent when they were expelled from God's presence.

Daniel gives us possibly a case in point (see Daniel 10). After fasting and praying he was visited by an angel—perhaps Gabriel—who told of ongoing battles with the princes—satanic angels—of Persia and Greece. These were not taking place within human sight, but seemed nevertheless to relate to places of human habitation.

The third heaven—seen by Paul and John—is God's residence and is "far above all the heavens" (Ephesians 4:10). This is where God has seated Jesus at His right hand "in the heavenly places, far above all rule and authority and power and dominion, and every name that is named" (Ephesians 1:20–21).

Job 22:14 (KJV) says that God walks "in the circuit of heaven." I take this to mean that heaven is a sphere like our earth. Its size is unknown, but *big*, bigger even than the second heaven, which holds a "countless" number of stars (see Jeremiah 33:22). If heaven is up in all directions and a sphere, perhaps it encircles our universe in some fashion.

From Revelation 21:16 we learn that the capital city of heaven, the New Jerusalem, is 1,500 miles long, wide and high. This city would cover about half of the United States—from Maine to Florida and from the Atlantic Ocean to the Colorado River. Though some believe it to be cube-shaped, I like Dr. H. A. Ironside's interpretation that the heavenly Jerusalem is shaped like a pyramid. I imagine it with the throne at the top. "The glory of God gives it light, and the Lamb is its lamp" (Revelation 21:23, NIV).

Out of the throne and down the middle of the street flows "a river of the water of life, clear as crystal. . . . And on either side of the river [is] the tree of life" (Revelation 22:1–2).

I have seen a tree more glorious than the white birch in Aspen or the jacaranda in Florida. I saw the Tree of Life during my 28-minute death experience and visit to heaven. I want to keep my passport in order—and Jesus is the way.

Twelve gates are positioned in the wall around the city, each a single pearl (see Revelation 21:21). The gates allow people to enter the city or to go out into what we might consider countryside. The walls around the city consist of twelve layers of gems: sapphires (blue), emeralds (green), sardonyx (pale blue), chrysolite (blue-green), beryl (pale green), topaz (golden yellow), amethyst (purple) and others mentioned in Revelation 21. God promises us that in exchange for sins forgiven and purity here, we will walk on gems. Satan has deceived the world to sell itself short for temporary riches. Jesus wants us to remember where our true riches lie.

A Most Wonderful Place

Where is heaven? It is the place where God is on the throne and Jesus sits at His right hand. It is the place from which the ultimate destiny of earth is being directed. Not only are the matters of the universe ordered and history brought to its final stage, but as Mona Johnian puts it in her Bible study of heaven: "God is ordering life in the heavenly realm, a lot of action more significant than we see here on earth." All authority in heaven and on earth is there. It could be that during Christ's millennial reign on earth we will have ready access to this governing capital.

The Holy Spirit is God's personal proof that heaven is real. Though no one has ever seen Him, He is called the Comforter, the Prompter, the One called alongside to help. He is the signal that Jesus arrived at the place where He told us He was going (see Acts 2:32–33). Just as Jesus has a glorified body (see Luke 24:36–43), we, too, will have glorified bodies in heaven. These will be our natural bodies "permanentized." Sometimes we long to exchange our earthly "tent" for that clothing of heaven (see 2 Corinthians 5:1–3).

Heaven is Paradise under God's monarchy. A teacher in Fort Wayne said of heaven: "I've been in a most wonderful place. The next time I go, don't bring me back."

Oden Hetrick, who told me about the beautiful robes he saw, described Paradise this way: "The sky was gold. So many things there were gold. It seemed to be the central color scheme. I went for a swim in the River of Life to wash off the last of earth's dust. I swam and splashed without effort. It was more like playing in a park. The river was deep, over my head, but I could breathe underwater. It covered all my scars of sin. The past remorse of my memory was buried there so I could forget it, too, and enjoy heaven. After that washing I felt worthy to be there. . . . I knew that earth was a mere shadow of heaven. I knew this was Jesus' home and saw many people who had died. I didn't want to return to earth."

Wherever heaven is, being there is like being in no other place. I am glad, however, that we do not have to wait until we get to heaven to get all of heaven. God has given us a foretaste of our inheritance. Look at the following letter, for instance.

Two days after reading your book Angels by My Side *an angel appeared suddenly to me in my bedroom and spoke three words: "Do not fear." Two days later while riding to the hospital coughing up blood hemorrhaged from my lungs, I felt no fear at any time. Four days later when I was released from the hospital there was some old blood in my right lung. Now, two weeks later, there is no evidence of any problem at all.*

The book of Isaiah contains this promise: "Before they call I will answer." God had prepared this woman with a little of heaven beforehand to remove her fear.

When we believe in Jesus we, too, have access to heaven on earth through His glorious presence. And someday He will take us to that place far above all we know to dwell with Him forevermore.

5

How Do We Feel about Heaven?

I did a telecast recently with C. M. Ward and asked him, "How can a person be sure he or she is going to heaven?"

"Easy," he replied with a smile. "By one word, *looking*. Think about these Scriptures: 'Unto them that look for him shall he appear the second time . . . unto salvation' (Hebrews 9:28, KJV) and 'I will guide thee with mine eye' (Psalm 32:8, KJV). You can receive intimate eye signals only if you have good eye contact and are paying attention to Him."

I think he is right. Living a few miles away from Carl and me is a man with three stretch limos, a gorgeous, faithful wife, four nice children and a lover in England. He is not looking for Jesus; he thinks this is heaven. It is my guess that a lot of people who are blasé about heaven are going to be disappointed that they did not spend more time thinking about it and about what it takes to get there.

My husband pastors a church in Dunedin, Florida. Last summer his associate, Karen Siddle, treated a young family visiting her to a day at Disney World. Driving home after a fun-packed day, the parents were appreciative, the younger children were happily exhausted and had fallen asleep. But the older boy sat looking out the window.

Karen asked him, "Well, Pete, what do you think?"

He answered blandly, "Is that all?"

People miss out on a lot of joy in this world by wrong attitudes. Most of us fail to get excited about heaven the way this boy was unimpressed by Disney World. For the individual who is going to heaven, nothing should stir up more enthusiasm. Earthly disappointments are one thing, but heaven cannot be a disappointment. No matter how wonderful we think it will be, it will be more wonderful still. There are too many churchgoers who have been singing the song "Redeemed" for 58 years, but not hearing the words!

I had an experience similar to Karen's but with a different outcome. About three winters ago, I brought a young mother of three small boys to Florida for six days. My husband was traveling and her mother-in-law took care of the little fellows.

She had never seen the ocean, never been out of her home state or flown in an airplane! I received more rest, relaxation and pure joy by showing her things she had never seen than I have for a long time. The remarks of appreciation and expressions of merriment on her face were more rewarding than I can describe.

Think how it must give the Lord pleasure when His children think about heaven with eager anticipation! If we enjoy sharing what we have with others, His delight in sharing the joys of heaven with us must know no bounds.

My Aunt Lillian was the principal of an elementary school in Indiana. Many of her students were poor farm children and offspring of riverboat folks. When one little fellow missed school most of the winter she visited his house to learn they had no heat and had burned most of their furniture in an old stove to keep warm. She went home and got help to carry her own couch and chair back to them. When she arrived, the little boy looked at his mother and squealed, "Mommy, this is like heaven!"

Can you imagine the utter joy, the wonder and amazement of children arriving in heaven from the underprivileged, starving nations of the world or the countries where people are tortured for their faith?

How different things are in our prosperous lands! I worked for five years in a jewelry store in New Castle, Indiana, and watched people comb the aisles to find something for a relative that he or she did not already have. One couple told me, "Our grandchildren still have presents in the basement unopened from last year." Some people are so engrossed with the baubles of this world they will miss the glories of the world to come.

We should be excited about heaven! It is the finish line, the end of the race where rewards and trophies will be given. Jesus said, "Be thou faithful unto death, and I will give thee a crown of life" (Revelation 2:10, KJV). In Jesus' Parable of the Talents, the master said, "Well done, thou good and faithful servant: thou hast been faithful over a few things, I will make thee ruler over many things: enter thou into the joy of thy lord" (Matthew 25:21, KJV).

Five "No Mores"

I like to enhance my perspective of heaven by thinking of it as a place of "no more." Here are five "no mores" that top my list.

No More Emergencies

First, heaven is a place of no more emergencies. No more death, sorrow or sickness. (I met a "little old lady" in the hospital. Her name was Ida Ill and she said, "With a name like that,

I've been sick all my life!" Then I saw an epitaph on a tombstone in Milwaukee that said, "I told you I was sick!")

I am a survivor. I have been through many storms in my life, and I have always found that God is faithful. I am glad that Jesus is in the prayer-answering business in heaven.

A pastor wrote me: "I was with an elderly woman who was dying. She asked me to pray that God would let her die. I hated to do it, so she prayed: 'I have been faithful, Lord. You have answered a lot of my living prayers; now answer this dying one. Lord, give me a new body. I can't stand this pain. I can't take this sickness any longer.' She quit breathing within five minutes."

Jesus has given us the best of both worlds. In our earthly lives He is working full-time to be our caring Father. He does not have a second job or other part-time employment, and we never have to worry about putting too much work on Him. When we have any problem, any emergency that we cannot handle, we can turn to Him.

And in our "heavenly" lives, there will be no emergencies to worry about. No wrong decisions, accidents, carelessness or evil to hurt us.

No More Unforgiveness

Second, heaven is a place of no more unforgiveness.

A young couple brought their seven-year-old daughter, Heather, to meet me and sent her out to play while they told me an amazing story.

The little girl had dived into the deep end of their backyard swimming pool, and they found her floating face down. Paramedics arrived in three or four minutes. In the emergency room of the hospital after a miraculous recovery from death, Heather gave her mother a curious message. She looked at her mother and said, "Grandma says she forgives you." Heather had never seen even a photograph of her grandmother, but was able to describe her—her size, her hair, the mole near her left ear.

Heather's mother told me she was taken aback at this message. She had become pregnant with Heather out of wedlock, and when her parents learned of it, they dismissed her from their home and told her never to return. A year later, after she had married and the little girl had been born, she tried to locate her parents only to learn they had moved. She destroyed all photos of her parents and hate festered in her heart for years.

Then she became born again and wanted to let her parents know she forgave them for their harsh rejection; Jesus had forgiven her fornication and she hoped they would, too. She and her husband began to pray for her parents' salvation.

Finally, soon after the drowning incident, they were able to locate her father and learned that her mother had died four weeks previously.

This young mother was able to put her heart at rest because of the unusual message her daughter brought back from heaven.

Forgiveness is the order of the day in heaven. Perhaps we will understand as never before the enormous gift of forgiveness that God has given us through His Son, Jesus Christ, and our own grievances will seem petty in the light of that love.

No More Pollution

Third, heaven is a place of no more pollution.

This does not just mean the pollution of our oceans and rivers and air. It includes the pollution in our nations of drugs, alcohol, greed, perversion.

I read an article this year about a teenager in Finland who is suing his parents for a million dollars because he says they brought him into this world without his consent to a life he feels is painful and fraught with hardship. An attorney, Erkki Kantola, said, "He may just have a case."

Other stories closer to home tell of hate and murder in families and neighborhoods.

Thank God there will be no sexual perversion (see Romans 1:26–29; 1 Corinthians 6:9–10). Jesus can break the chains of deception and release the captives from that prison. "Such were some of you: but ye are washed . . . sanctified . . . justified in the name of the Lord Jesus, and by the Spirit of our God" (1 Corinthians 6:11, KJV).

His blood can cleanse from all sin, but we must want the change. We must quit our sin. Then we can enjoy the purity of heaven, the unpolluted thoughts and actions awaiting us there.

No More Unsung Heroes

Fourth, heaven is a place of no more unsung heroes.

Heaven will reveal a different perspective on accomplishments. I am anxiously awaiting awards night up there. We will have eternity to stage many awards sessions for the faithful, the anonymous, the people whose integrity has been consistent—the *always* people. Here we tend to applaud the rich and famous; there everyone gets his just and earned rewards.

I love snow at Christmas, but I lived in the Dakotas where we had snow on the ground for about eight months out of the year. We had two seasons: July and winter.

Those sturdy Dakotans are real people, loving their families and working to grow grain for us where there are few trees and the wind chill factor zooms down to 125 degrees below zero. One year the temperature was below zero for 64 days. In heaven the Dakotans will probably live in the southern clime on the sunny side! "For God is not unrighteous to forget your work and labour of love, which ye have shewed toward his name, in that ye have ministered to the saints, and do minister" (Hebrews 6:10, KJV).

First Corinthians 12:28 speaks of the ministry of "helps." What a great career, though it is not heralded much in this life!

Likewise with counseling, exhorting (which means encouraging), serving, giving, showing mercy. In heaven, the people who have been about these occupations will be properly honored and rewarded.

My friend Sara Douglas was a giver. I am sure she is an administrator in the "Giving Department" up there. She was always giving fruit, flowers, books, clothes, time on the phone and useful reading materials here. I have no doubt that Esther Zink and Paul and Mona Johnian will be executives in heaven's great book and tape library. They have shared their materials unselfishly and generously.

I know two women who do not want to reveal their names, but who have prayed for a Dakota boy for 22 years. He is now a gifted neurosurgeon. When they all get to heaven, those two will share in his rewards.

No More Unfulfilling Work

Fifth, heaven is a place of no more stressful, unhappy or unfulfilling work. God created work and it is good. When Adam and Eve sinned in the Garden, however, work turned into grueling labor.

It is true that many people have jobs they enjoy. This is something of a mirror image of the way work was meant to be. These people marvel that they receive payment for jobs they would do without any reimbursement.

For the most part, however, this is not the case. Many women, for instance, have been deserted by their husbands and left alone to support their children. Many men find it hard to pay bills on meager salaries.

In heaven we can rest from our labors. I believe there will be work there, but it will be the kind of labor that invigorates us, that thrills us with its fulfillment. It will be the thing we love doing most, and we will do it for the honor of our Lord Jesus.

Other "No Mores"

These, I think, are the top five, but there are plenty of other "no mores" in heaven.

No more racing the clock. We will have all of eternity to accomplish our goals, our deepest desires. We will get everything done.

No more separation from the Prince of Peace. There will be political harmony, for the government will be upon His shoulders. No war, no weapons, no fear of attack from another nation.

And there are still more! Look at this list:

no more hurricanes	no more stress	no more fear
no more separation	no more weeds	no more sin
no more storms	no more thorns	no more worry
no more limitations	no more night	no more locks
no more cancer	no more want	no more pain
no more tears	no more clocks	no more medicine
no more judgment	no more decay	no more guilt
no more alcohol abuse	no more bad habits	no more drugs

A mother wrote me from Washington state that in a dream she saw her son for whom she was grieving. He told her, "Don't wish me back. You forget I was born blind. I am *seeing* the wonders of glory here." She said her grieving ended.

I have heard that Billy Graham had a vision of his grandfather who had lost a leg and an eye in the Civil War. He was complete, walking and seeing.

And I spoke with a handicapped man who has been frail since birth. He said that during prayer one morning he was given a vision of sporting events in heaven. It was thrilling to see, he said, because an athlete's body is not hindered there and can reach its greatest potential with God's power and strength.

Walking along among the athletes, he noticed a young man, his marvelous back muscles flexing as he threw the shot put. When the athlete turned, the man saw it was *his* face! He is looking forward to heaven with an eager perspective because he believes he will be there what he always wanted to be here.

All puzzles complete . . . all missing parts restored better than new. We shall stand complete in Him!

A New Perspective

Does this undergird your perspective about heaven? It does mine! And it tells me something else: While people can change our perspectives about heaven, heaven changes our perspectives about people.

When my life was coming to a screeching halt in that hospital room, I recalled the saying, "You can't take it with you." I had never been sick. Now I lay dying and realized that I had never liked people, but that people—those we help find salvation—are all we can take with us to eternity. When God gave me a second chance to live, I returned with a new perspective: the desire to invest in people. "People" are the only commodity that transfers from this life to the next.

From its creation, heaven has been a marvelous, complete place, always inhabited with angels and palatial splendor. But from the beginning God wanted something more. He wanted people to be there, too.

People are important to Him. He does not wish that any should perish (see 2 Peter 3:9). God the Father created people; Jesus died for people; the Holy Spirit indwells people.

We all know those who have invested in people. I once got a letter written in a feeble hand. The old man asked, "Do you know of any pill to cure loneliness?" For some time my Aunt

Gwen corresponded with him. He loved to get something in his mailbox.

The same day I got his letter, I got a letter from Sue Sharp in Kentucky. She said she felt a prompting in her heart to drive across town and check on an elderly friend. She started to shrug it off because it meant battling afternoon rush-hour traffic, but her heart would not let her ignore it. She arrived to find her friend too incapacitated to reach for the phone and summon help.

As we invest in people we realize that we are many times on the receiving end of others' investments. One day, while carrying two cartons of blooming plants down the path home, I met Carolyn.

"Honey," she said, "tell me that you didn't *buy* those." She took me to her house. "My yard is overgrown with anything that grows in Florida." Now my yard looks like Eden. She has given me some of everything she has.

Carolyn has a wonderful perspective on helping others. Early one morning I decided to walk my three miles before it got too hot. There was Carolyn down on the beach picking up trash. I asked her if she were the beach angel.

"No," she said, "I'm the original bag lady. I come every morning and evening and tidy up the beach. While I'm here I get to enjoy the sunrise and sunset. I don't guess I've missed a single one in twenty-six years."

This woman lives alone but is never lonely. She has a merry heart, and in giving of herself, she receives enjoyment from the beauty of the world around her.

Little things can mean a lot when we invest in others. Last February I sent a valentine to the most despised, hateful, selfish woman in the state of Illinois. I met her some time ago and her miserable reputation of greed has followed her for many years.

I was amazed to receive a note from her. She wrote, "This is the first valentine I have gotten since I was a girl thirteen years old." It broke her heart. Her neighbors tell me she has made a drastic change since then.

Our perspectives on heaven and the people we help to find it are important to the way we live our lives now. We can keep that perspective aligned by praising Jesus for the joy of eternity with Him, and by sharing the Good News with others.

Few things are more exciting!

6

Hell: The Involuntary Alternative

Satan never minds if you talk about him or his domain. He has not a care in the world if you "mean mouth" him—so long as you forget to talk to God. I refuse to give Satan free advertisement on a page of this book, but I do not think one can write adequately about heaven without mentioning the involuntary alternative, hell, which is also a permanent dwelling place.

One man wrote me: "My veins collapsed for the third time after a heart attack. Light and dark waged a war. Suddenly all was black as night in the Carlsbad Caverns in New Mexico when tourists are taken underground and the lights are cut off for some moments. My spirit left my body—it felt like pulling the stopper out of a thermos bottle. Faster and faster it traveled at what felt like a 45-degree angle. I saw horrors, undescribable pitch blackness. I thought, *This must be hell. . . .*"

The Scriptures are plain: "Do not be deceived, God is not mocked; for whatever a man sows, this he will also reap" (Galatians 6:7). "All have sinned and fall short of the glory of God"

(Romans 3:23). We are lost unless we cling to the saving grace of Jesus. As the hymn says,

> My hope is built on nothing less
> Than Jesus' blood and righteousness. . . .
> His oath, His covenant, His blood,
> Support me in the whelming flood.
> Edward Mote (1797–1874)

When we were children, Mother used to tell us, "If you never play with matches, you'll never burn the house down." It followed: "If you don't try smoking, you'll never have to kick the habit. . . . If you never taste alcohol, you'll never become a drunkard."

We used to play a game called "First he took a nibble, then he took a bite." Sin is like that. It seems innocent or insignificant at first, but if it is left unchecked or not repented of, it can lead to the loss of your soul. Satan does not announce his motive to damn our souls. He tries to deceive us into sinning and to bluff us into thinking there's no way out. Beware: There is no right way to do wrong.

In some parts of India people worship snakes. Many people refuse to kill them. I saw a newspaper article describing how one came into a home and coiled around the neck of a six-month-old baby. The child was found dead. Serpents of sin—drunkenness, pride, adultery—are slipping into our homes whenever we open the door to them even a crack.

Some interpret God's mercy to mean that He will never send a soul to hell. They are not considering that God is a righteous Judge. Suppose the governor of a state could not bear to see anyone punished for breaking the law and pardoned everyone the courts convicted. He would not be governor for long. The state would be unsafe.

God has certain laws, too. He has told us clearly that we must repent of our sins (see Acts 17:30) and believe in the Lord Jesus

Christ (see Romans 10:9) in order to be saved. Scripture says that "whoever believes in Him will not be disappointed" (Romans 10:11). Those who do not believe in Him will be.

I spent some time with Dr. Maurice Rawlings, a heart specialist and author of *Beyond Death's Door*. He told me that of the patients whose deaths he witnessed, 80 percent had a horrible experience and only 20 percent had a peaceful experience. Jesus said, "Enter by the narrow gate; for the gate is wide, and the way is broad that leads to destruction, and many are those who enter by it. For the gate is small, and the way is narrow that leads to life, and few are those who find it" (Matthew 7:13–14).

Dr. Rawlings also said that while people described hellish experiences immediately upon returning to life, they later seemed to forget them or put them out of their minds. He said, "The evil god of this world, Satan, has blinded their eyes so they cannot remember and warn others."

But some have had their lives changed by the experience and have warned us. Dr. George Ritchie has written of the desolation he felt at being asked: "What did you do with your life?" The deeds he had thought to be so important seemed minuscule under the scrutiny of that question.

He saw miserable people writhing in agony trying to make up to their living loved ones for hurts they had caused. He saw people chained to the consequences of their behaviors, for all eternity powerless to satisfy themselves. He saw people fighting, gouging each other, but never dying, howling with despair.

Then in the distance he saw a light—Jesus, the Light of the world. He returned to life and had a second chance to tell others about Jesus.

Here are some last words of famous people.

Voltaire, an atheist, spent his last few months in such remorse and fear of hell that his nurse said she would never again attend a dying atheist.

Edward Gibbon, philosopher, author of *The Decline and Fall of the Roman Empire* and an infidel, died with these words: "All is now lost, finally irrecoverably lost. All is dark and doubtful."

Atheist Thomas Hobbes died in Devonshire, England, saying: "I am about to take a leap in the dark, and I shall be glad to find a hole [into which] to creep out of the world's misery."

Cardinal Beaufort Winchester, half-brother to King Henry IV, said these last words: "And must I then die? Will not my riches save me? I could purchase the kingdom if that would prolong my life. Alas, there is no bribing death!"

Sir Francis Newport was dying as a young man. "Wretch that I am," he said, "what will become of me?" An infidel companion tried to dispel his fears but he replied, "There is a God, I know. I am equally sure there is a hell. All sins are brought to my remembrance. I was religiously educated so my torment is greater than if I had not known. Oh, the insufferable pangs of hell!"

Ethan Allen, a noted infidel, wrote a book against the divinity of the Lord. His wife, a devoted Christian, died leaving a young daughter who became the idol of her father. Now the daughter was dying of tuberculosis. He begged her not to die, but she replied, "Doctor says I will die today. Mother told me about the Savior who died for us all and He sits enthroned in glory. Shall I accept Him as she did, or reject Him as you have taught me?"

Speaking through tears, Allen replied, "My child, cling to your mother's Savior. She was right. I'll try to follow you to that blessed abode."

We, too, must seek Him while He may be found. God has one Son. He lived a sinless life on this earth, died at Calvary and conquered death by rising from the grave. The Holy Spirit is our Comforter, the One alongside us to help us choose to follow Jesus.

Once flying from Tampa I fell asleep and woke to hear the attendant announce: "After a brief stop in Dallas, this plane will continue to Phoenix. Unless you are continuing with this flight, you must deplane."

Because of our sins, we are headed like passengers on a plane for one destination: hell. But we can choose to "deplane" and repent of the lives we are living and take a flight for another destination. Not making the change is the same as choosing to remain off course. If you are headed in the wrong direction, repent and transfer before it is too late.

Sara Douglas shared a dream with me recently from years before that had changed her life. She dreamed she was in a reception hall. Most of her friends were there, but she had a dreadful feeling she should not be. They were glad she was with them, but there was no gladness in her heart. When she awakened, she began searching for the Way, and found it.

On earth gravity pulls everything down. In heaven everything is up—up toward the throne of God, bounding upward with spiritual gravitation. Just as there are two poles to a magnet, positive and negative, so all souls will be drawn toward one of two places. God's throne is the center of His everlasting Kingdom of light, and toward it all gracious spirits who are blood-washed are drawn from the time they accept Jesus.

In heaven there is all life and no death. In hell there is all death and no life. Here on earth we have both living and dying, which stand between the two. If we are dead to sin here, we have truly begun to live.

7

The Journey Starts Here

I love to ponder this saying: "The journey to the house of a friend is never long." That is, I love to ponder it in relation to Jesus. "What a Friend we have in Jesus!" the hymn proclaims. We are on our way on the journey to heaven and can rejoice even if the going gets bumpy now and then. The goal makes the journey worthwhile.

My new word processor, to give an example, has made the journey through this book bumpy, but I am not distracted because I have a goal. One morning I had a chapter completed ready to save and print out. The phone rang and I took my eyes from the main road onto a short side trip. Consequently, I pushed the wrong buttons—and wiped out the chapter. Later that day a man came to the door and I locked myself out of my writing studio. I lost two hours of work, thirty dollars for a locksmith and, rushing upstairs to get the money, I fell, turned my ankle, bruised my elbow and howled pitifully.

But I got up and kept going because I have a goal that means more to me than any inconvenience along the way.

Last year I traveled more than 150,000 miles on many, many trips. After each one several people would ask the same question: "How was your trip?" The answer was usually the same: I was glad to be home, particularly from the rough rides.

Our journey to heaven is like this. Heaven is our ultimate goal, our long-awaited home, and we can anticipate our arrival on each day of our journey through this life. It does not matter where you come from, but it does matter where you are going and how you get there. God cares only that you walk with Him.

Having a Safe Trip

Here are six principles we can follow to enhance the journey, to be assured that we walk with Him.

The Walk

First, we must "walk our talk."

For Christmas Carl and I both got navy-and-orange sweat-shirts from Wheaton College where our daughter April is captain of the women's basketball team. All over the back of the sweatshirts are footprints and the slogan: *Walk your talk: Job 22:22.* She had been appointed designer of the warm-up sweats and wanted to convey this idea from Scripture: Obey the rules, keep them in your heart, and the Lord will be your defense. In other words, "Don't just talk about basketball; play the game." Talk is cheap. It is what you do, the follow-through, that counts.

On our journey to heaven we must "walk our talk" as well. Satan is going to do all he can to trip us, so it is vital to keep our hearts on Jesus and our minds on the goal: heaven.

Last year I spoke at a lovely church in Alberta, Canada, pastored by Wally Reihl. It was near Eastertide, and when I described my death experience we had no idea how close Wally was to the end of his journey.

I received a letter from his wife, Erica, recently and she told me how Wally had preached two sermons, his last two it turned out, on heaven. Then he suffered a heart attack and died shortly after.

Erica said she wore white to the funeral instead of black. "It is not time to focus on lonely me," she wrote, "but to point people to Jesus, to heaven, the place where Wally waits."

Wally walked his talk. He was a Christian—a "little Christ"— naturally and sincerely. He made the journey pleasant for his wife, his children and his church. And in his death, Erica showed another example of walking with God on the journey.

Loving Life

Second, we should love life along the journey.

Sometimes we need to slow down and sip, not gulp, as we go along the way. I get aggravated when people damn this world. The Bible says that God declared His creation good. The apostle Paul wrote that "since the creation of the world [God's] invisible attributes, His eternal power and divine nature, have been clearly seen, being understood through what has been made" (Romans 1:20).

I have started riding my bike or walking to the post office each morning. If it rains, I enjoy listening to the pleasant patter on the umbrella. This allows me to hear the birds, see the blooming flowers, smile at people and receive their greetings in their kind voices.

Bill Van Garven lived across the street from us in North Dakota. He works at the post office—hard and fast all day. But when he can he retreats to the woods to help him slow his pace and regain his love for life. He sent me this:

> It's miraculous how the serenity of trying to spot elusive white-
> tails along a wooded creek or a patient walk through the soft,

pleasant atmosphere of nature drains all the tension and confusing thoughts from a person's mind. All the elements of nature work like a prescribed medicine to lift your spirits and cleanse your frustrated soul. After only a few deep breaths and several minutes among the oaks and willows, you're freed of society's grasping control.

You soon forget about money pressures, social problems, the unmowed lawn or the broken window in the garage. Gradually a smile spreads across your face as you begin to feel positive about life, about yourself. You feel sympathy toward those who haven't the desire or time to experience this simple gift. And when you leave the life-giving woodlands and return to the concrete world, you can hold your head high and walk with a lively step.

If we take the time to love life we will find the Creator a ready Companion on our walks toward heaven.

Finding Rest

Third, we should release our burdens to Jesus along the way. Jesus said, "Come to Me, and I will give you rest for the journey." You will find that the cares might not disappear, but the burden of the cares and work will.

I have found that burdened spirits often lead to physical problems—notably, for some reason, with digestion. I do not think our systems can work properly if we try to carry a load too heavy for them. We need to learn to rest in our Father's ability to take our trials and bring us security. He will enable us to prevail in every situation. After we receive His rest, we can perform our responsibilities and continue the journey toward the goal.

Not all burdens have to be big important ones in order to weigh us down. Small frustrations affect us, too. If you think little things have little meaning, trying pulling your thumb out of a noose of sticky tape or tripping on a shoestring while you are jogging! It is not usually the big mountains in our paths that make life hard; it is often the small pebbles in our shoes.

We know there are rewards in heaven in exchange for our burdens, but there are often rewards on the journey.

My first baby had colic. The only reason I did not lose my mind or sell her for 59 cents plus tax was the fact that Dr. Ben Harrison assured me it would only last three to six months. Naturally, I am glad I persevered! She has brought me 35 years of pride and joy.

History hurrahs David for defeating Goliath. It was a risk, but someone had to do it—and it seems that no one else was even considering how to go about it. David, appalled that anyone should so reproach the God of Israel, gambled, put his faith in God and won. It was a simple battle, just his faith in God and a rock.

And David's valor was not without rewards—pleasures for the journey. First Samuel 17:25 tells us that whoever killed the giant would receive great riches and the king's daughter as a bride, and would never have to pay taxes again for the rest of his life. (I would almost join the army for that last benefit. Have you paid Florida taxes lately?)

It will help us on the journey to remember that even Jesus "for the joy set before Him endured the cross, despising the shame" (Hebrews 12:2). He remained faithful during His walk on earth because He knew heaven was waiting for Him at the end of His journey here.

Scripture says:

> Let us hold fast the confession of our hope without wavering, for He who promised is faithful. . . . Therefore, do not throw away your confidence, which has a great reward. For you have need of endurance, so that when you have done the will of God,

you may receive what was promised. For yet in a very little while, He who is coming will come, and will not delay.

Hebrews 10:23, 35–37

Traveling Companions

Fourth, as we move forward on the journey we should take someone with us.

I read an article in which Peggy Karey told this story. She was hurrying through a railway station and barely paused to toss a coin into the hat of a crippled man who was selling pencils. Then she stopped, went back and asked for her pencil. "He wasn't a beggar," she wrote. "He was a businessman."

Some months later she bought a book at a newsstand in the same station. "I've been looking for you," the owner said to her. She recognized him as the man who had been selling pencils. "You were the first person who ever treated me like a businessman, and now you can see what your encouragement meant to me. I *am* a businessman."

The way we treat each other is vitally important. In fact, our future life in heaven reflects our choices in this life—the bundle of relationships we develop. Hence, this present life is really the only place where we can determine what type of life we will enjoy in the next real world.

Carl, from his theological/pastoral perspective, puts it this way:

The end of the age as described in the Word of God is to be marked by judgment, Tribulation and destruction, and finally the earth itself being renovated by fire. The apocalyptic vision itself serves as a catalyst for every Christian: "The earth passeth away and the fashion thereof, but he that doeth the will of God abideth forever." In the light of this revelation we see the sinners around us—the unsaved of the world—unwarned, unaware that time is merging for them into a crisis eternity. Every footstep in time has an echo in eternity, and just as those in Kora's rebellion found eternity beneath their feet (an earthquake swallowed them), and David, too, recognized that he was but a step from death. Time's form is "now" but time's substance is eternal.

The choice is "now" but the results of that choice are eternal.

The opportunity for reaching souls is "now." The results of our efforts or our failure will be eternal.

Evangelist Lowell Lundstrom was one of the few ministers I know who never closed a service without inviting people to receive Jesus and salvation.

His journey began in Peever, South Dakota, population 104. There was a gas station, a feed store and a tavern. Lowell spent every Saturday evening until dark peeping into the doorway of that bar watching a man play a guitar. By watching the fingering closely, he was able to learn to play. Later he was born again and chose to play his guitar to worship the Lord and lead others to Him.

My dad's journey required some hard choices, too. During the Depression he had to quit college. Jobs could not be found. For a while we lived with my grandparents. Then when my baby brother Don was born, we moved into an old run-down country house that we could fix up for free rent. One time all we had to eat for two days was one boiled potato.

One morning Mother grew worried when she saw Dad take his last shotgun shell and head for the woods. When she heard the shot she was terrified that he might have taken his life. Five minutes later she learned that as he contemplated ending his failure as a provider, the skinniest rabbit you ever saw ran across his path. We had boiled rabbit for three days.

Eventually my father pioneered nine small churches that he built with his own hands.

When I lay in a coma, Art Lindsey from Toad Hop, Indiana, population 48, came and read the Word to me. Since then he has become a prison chaplain and has won many to the Lord.

Small miracles grow into larger ones. God uses ordinary people when He gets ready to do something extraordinary. We should not frown on the journey. Smith Wigglesworth said, "We must look at earth's problems from heaven's standpoint."

We can do little things for each other to encourage ourselves in our walks with God. Most of my driving is along Highway 19. It reminds me of the battle of Armageddon: Sometimes there are four wrecks in the space of a mile. It is frightening—and maddening always to be stuck in a lane behind the latest crash, but once in a while someone will have compassion on you and let you in line. Little things like that, little sacrifices, can help us be grateful for others and reach out in return.

One hot July I was invited to speak at a conference in Arizona for six days, and wondered at first why they had not invited me to come in February instead! The temperature ranged from 105 to 115 degrees. But the journey! The people I stayed with were a tonic, so pleasant. And let me tell you about my sneakers.

For the trip to Arizona I packed three pairs of high heels and washed my old "holes-in-the-toes" Reeboks to take along, too. (I had rescued them from the garbage once when April threw them away.) I put the shoes on the porch to dry and figured I would remember them since I practically had to stumble over them coming out of the door.

Well, while hurrying to the airport I missed them. In Arizona I told my hostess, Barbara Nelson, that I needed to buy a pair of walking shoes. I did not mention that I did not have the money for them, but hoped that somewhere along the line from a love offering I would.

That same morning in the prayer breakfast I saw a woman hand Barbara a pair of Reebok walking shoes exactly like my old worn ones at home—but these were brand new.

The two women came over to me and I joked, "Are those in case you run out of gas and have to walk home?"

"No," the woman said. "These are for you. They arrived this morning and I wondered if you had any use for them."

It so happened that the woman's brother was stationed in Korea near the Reebok factory. She had asked him to send her a pair, size 9. He had mailed her a size 8—my size—by mistake.

Along the journey, God planned a beautiful pair of shoes in my size to arrive from Korea just when I would be in Arizona and need them. They had arrived right on time for me!

As we care for others, God makes sure we are cared for ourselves as we walk the journey from here to there.

Humorous Interludes

Fifth, we should make full use of our enthusiasm and humor. These qualities are all around us, and how they liven up the journey! I spoke at Zion Bible College in Barrington, Rhode Island, for graduation weekend. The topic of our dinner conversation turned toward heaven and led to this exchange.

Jack Mitchell's wife, Bert, asked him, "Jack, if I die before Jesus comes, will you remarry?"

With mischief in his smile, he responded, "Sure. You know I don't like to go to funerals by myself."

We hooted with laughter.

My husband, Carl, is 66. He is full of fun and enthusiasm. He wrote a book called *If You're Over the Hill, You Oughta Be Goin' Faster*. He wakes up early each morning looking for a fresh new challenge, another mountain to climb while pastoring his church and waiting for the Rapture.

I remember from my childhood many times, early morning, my grandpa Dad Perky would stand by the east window and whisper, "Maybe today!" His enthusiasm for heaven gave him enthusiasm for life.

I think my dad, who is full of the joy of life, will go out with gusto. He lives on my brother Jim's ranch. His favorite cow,

Tinker Bell, had been missing for four days. She is somewhere between 16 and 24 years old and caring for her is part of my father's loving routine.

Down a gravel road from him live some people who have gained a questionable reputation. When anything is missing, the sheriff usually finds it there.

Neighborhood ranchers were offering help by planning reports and strategies. My dad simply donned his purple and orange cap, walked down the rocky road to the rustlers' thicket, opened the gate and called, "Come on, Tinker Bell. Let's go home." She knew his voice. She and her calf followed him the whole way. It must have been some picture!

Living each day with enthusiasm is like being a child with a new toy.

Looking to Him

Sixth, we should keep our eyes on Jesus for every step of the journey.

David Mains tells the story about walking through a smelly garbage section of Montreal when, suddenly, he noticed a beautiful fragrance. Looking to the side he saw several girls from the perfume factory on a lunch break. They were permeated with the fragrance because of their constant exposure to it.

I believe we can be saturated with the light of Jesus, till people will sense where we have been, and where we are going.

We can be like the old song:

> Shut in with God in a secret place,
> There in the Spirit beholding His face;
> Gaining new power to run in life's race,
> I long to be shut in with God.

Shut in with Him, but not shutting people out in their need. Not isolated from reality, but insulated by a taste of the help Jesus is ready to give us, often through angels, His divinely appointed helpers. Look at these letters I have received about God helping people along the journey when they kept their eyes on Him:

> *Grandma took me and my three-year-old sister to McDonald's tonight. We were ten cents short of what we needed at the cash register. I bowed my head and prayed. Right there a man gave me a quarter, then he was gone, we couldn't find him. It might have been an angel, because the devil wouldn't bless God's children, would he?*
>
> *Love, Enosh, Tracie and*
> *Grandma Fee*

This one came from an eleven-year-old in Southboro, Massachusetts:

> *My mother, sister and I went swimming. I got away from them in an undertow. I could not scream for help because my face was pounding the ocean floor and my mouth was hurt and full of sand. I felt hands under my armpits pull me out and take me to my mother and sister on the shore. He was gone. There was no one else on the beach before or after but the three of us. I believe the Word. "It rains on the just and the unjust alike." I didn't know Jesus then. He watches over us even before we know Him. He saved my life, then my soul.*
>
> *Love, Helen*

This letter came from a professional fisherman in Alaska, Clarence Straits, who wrote me about an experience he had had while fishing rough waters on a hazardous day.

> *I was running the hydraulic winch that turns to pick up about 5,000 pounds of fish. I hooked the bag, had lifted it*

to the top of the rail, when we hit a wave and lost all but one scrap on the winch. There was no way I could have held that much fish there. It should have hurled me around the winch and through the rigging. Suddenly everything slowed down; a wave came and set the bag of fish back for me. There must have been an angel assisting.

Until He Comes

I grew up near the coalmining town of Rockville, Indiana, where my dad pastored. I do not know how those miners could go underground before daylight and come home after dark. And there were so many cave-ins. Many times my dad would go to the shaft and elevator door and stand in the rain and cold waiting for news after a shale slide, hoping for reports of "alive."

What kept them going on such a hard journey? They looked forward to attending an old-fashioned, Jesus-loving church where they found His joy to hold them from Sunday to Sunday with the hope of heaven up ahead. Love kept them down there, making a living for children and wives. One brawny picker told me, "The soul afraid of dying never frees up and learns to live." If we have our eyes on Jesus we cannot see fear at the same time.

Jesus said to occupy until He comes. Enjoy the journey! We should not just dream of heaven; we should do something on the journey until then. I believe He wants us to have a good life here. And we can start by teaching our next generation, if Jesus tarries, the old path of "seeking Him early." Seek Him early in a situation before it gets out of hand. Seek Him early each morning before we get sidetracked. Seek Him early in life while we are young, before the cares of life or deceitfulness of riches chokes us.

Abraham spent his entire life en route to the place where the builder and maker is God. His faith was attached to the capital city of heaven. Set your affections long range. Will the things worrying you now really trouble you six months from now?

We have all of eternity to celebrate the victories, but only a few hours before sunset to win them. And in the ages to come He will show us "the exceeding riches of his grace in his kindness toward us" (Ephesians 2:7, KJV).

Dawn Wagler, an artist/writer friend of mine, is writing a Mother's Day article on the sounds and smells of home. I remember the sounds from the kitchen of my mother when she was scraping the skillet, pouring the gravy. It was, she reminded us, the last thing before dinner was ready, our signal that it was time to come to the table. And when we arrived, the welcome aroma made us feel happy and fulfilled.

Now we can imagine that in heaven the Marriage Supper of the Lamb is being prepared. We are almost within sight of home, and soon we will get the call that all is ready.

"Come and sup with Me," He will say. And we will have arrived. The journey will be over.

8

Rehearsal for Heaven

When Carl and I were engaged to be married, he would sometimes call and ask to come over for dinner. I was never sure if he was lonely for a family, hungry for a home-cooked meal or checking me out to see if I could cook!

All afternoon before the five o'clock arrival of Carl and his little daughter, Connie, I would—along with cooking dinner—clean the house, groom my children, perfume my hair, burn incense in the dining room to camouflage the scorch smells, put a linen tablecloth on the table, fold napkins with the corners mitered to match those of an expensively wrapped Christmas present, light pale pink candles and wait for their arrival.

Carl did not arrive as an afterthought, bring his leftover charm, leftover energy, leftover time to me. He did not bark a menu of what he demanded to eat. He came looking and acting sharp, his best. He appreciated what I had chosen to prepare and serve.

Just as most married couples start out with true appreciation for one another, so we give our best to Jesus when we first come to know Him. And just as couples often hit what is called "an eight-year plateau," so we tend to level off in our relationship with Jesus. In the book of Revelation, we read that Jesus chastised a group of believers by saying, "I have this against you, that you have left your first love" (2:4).

Remember how excited you were when you first found Jesus, His love and forgiveness, His healing? How you started worshiping with other believers and became part of a church? This is what Revelation means about losing our first love. It is called backsliding. The heart of the Prodigal Son had traveled to that faraway country, away from his family and his God, long before his feet went there.

As I was growing up, Wednesday night was Bible study and testimony night in our church. My dad would walk down the aisle and ask, "Does anyone have a testimony, a witness for the Lord tonight? Maybe you've had an unusual experience or a prayer answered that you want to share to encourage others to believe to receive an answer to theirs."

One particular night my mother brought the house down with her testimony. She had had a dream.

"I have become entangled with fears, worry, concern about finances, children's communicable diseases and the cares of life in general," she told us, "until I have not been praying or reading my Bible the way I used to when I was first saved.

"I dreamed last night that Jesus came. I heard the trumpet blow announcing the Rapture. I was in the chicken yard near our orchard feeding cracked corn to our chickens. I didn't go up, so I started leaping and jumping and bouncing upward hoping to take off with the people I had seen rise.

"I looked up and my children and husband had a great head-start on me. I was both heartbroken and horror-struck, but I finally got off the ground. I soared above the apple orchard. I looked down—and suddenly I backslid and fell downward.

Lying on my back I heard the squawking of the hens and roosters crowing mockingly. I had fallen on my back and was in the chicken lot.

"When I awoke," she concluded, "I determined to revive my first love for Jesus and begin Rapture practice!"

When she told this I was only about seven years old, but I have never forgotten that story. God usually uses humor to minister truths ever so solemn to me.

I did not hear that expression *Rapture practice* again for 51 years until I saw it recently in a Christian newsletter I received. It showed a picture of a Victorian house with the sign out front reading *Estate Sale*. It represented the aftermath of the Rapture for those owners: They were dead and everything else was left behind.

Now, remember that we cannot practice for the Rapture—that great gathering and transporting of believers to heaven (see 1 Thessalonians 4:16–18)—by storing up treasures here on earth. One day all our keepsakes—all the things we put into closets, into vaults and on to our curio shelves—will be left behind. Only the treasures of love, the hours spent in prayer and daily devotions, the wisdom we store from the Bible will go with us beyond this life.

We still have time to rehearse for the future—to clean out our closets, to hold only loosely on to our possessions and valuables, to concentrate on durable riches, lasting treasures. It is almost enough to make you want to go out to the backyard and practice jumping up and down!

The Scriptures tell us to lay aside every weight that would hold us back, and to get rid of everything that would sidetrack us (see Hebrews 12:1–2). The Phillips translation of these verses says we should get rid of the sins that "dog our feet." An apt description!

The King James Version calls them things that "so easily beset us." That could also mean the things that so easily *upset* us, like people not returning books we lent them, cranky salespersons or following people who let the doors slam in our faces. Our attitudes are so important. Think how many opportunities we have to add new treasures to our heavenly store!

If Jesus were coming tomorrow morning, would you make any major changes in the way you live today? Are you ready?

Just after hurricane Elena hit here in 1985, I saw a man interviewed on the local news. He lived in a trailer court and had been standing, naked as the day he was born, shaving in front of his medicine cabinet mirror. The winds ripped off the side of his mobile home, leaving him standing there shaken, but virtually unharmed. "They kept warning us," he said, "but I didn't believe it."

I have watched my children cram for a test or practice too late for a piano recital. They barely made a good showing approaching their responsibilities like this. I believe the race is run best in a sure and steady way.

A woman in England, bedridden for many years, watched as a bird built a nest in a tree outside her window. But it built the nest so low that she feared for its safety. Every day, as her little feathered friend structured the nest, the woman kept warning, "Build a little higher!" She knew that the bird was likely to come to grief.

At last it laid eggs and hatched them. She watched, concerned, while the mother brought food for her little ones. Then one morning she saw nothing but scattered feathers. A cat!

"It would have been a kindness if I had torn her nest down the first day," she lamented.

This is what God does for us very often. He snatches things away before it is too late.

Many who have fallen would love to go back before that time even for a brief moment. How differently they would guard their motives as they labored for the great end for which our

Lord suffered and died, and for which we are now practicing: heaven!

Many people, even in many churches, have forgotten that our real mission is to bring back the world to God. We are sometimes like the traveling salesman who gets so busy living it up that he forgets to sell his products—and loses his job. Our assignment is not to build a personal monument, but to lift up the name of the Son of the living God.

If we do not start now, it may soon be too late to join that great throng of those who are blood-washed, faithfully toiling while they wait to join the mighty host above.

I like the illustration D. L. Moody used about being water-logged. A friend of his told him of seeing a vessel being towed along the River Mersey and into the Liverpool harbor. It appeared to be so heavily laden he wondered why it did not sink.

Pretty soon another large vessel came steaming into the harbor without any need for assistance.

The friend made inquiry and learned that the first vessel was waterlogged. That is, it had sprung a leak and sunk partially, making it hard to bring in.

Many Christians have become waterlogged. They have laden themselves down with too many treasures, and it takes nearly the whole church to keep them afloat, to keep them from sinking into the world's riches. If we are not reaching the world, perhaps it is because we have more of the world in our hulls than we do of the grace and thoughts of God. We have too much earth and not enough heaven.

We get salvation as a free gift, but we have to work out how we choose to live in relation to it. If you inherited a diamond mine, you would have to work it to make it profitable.

When Paul's life was threatened, he never flinched. He did not write letters to defend himself, did not debate on television or try to justify himself or his mistakes. Instead, he said he would do it all over again for God. His only regret was that he did not start to serve God earlier, and that he had ever lifted his voice against the Lord.

I believe he went through the royal receiving line shouting, "Hallelujah! O my God! I bless Thee that I am in heaven at last!" His joy obliterated any remnants of earthly sorrow.

We cannot be selfish and unloving in one life and generous and loving in the next. The two lives are too closely blended, one a continuation of the other. We bring to heaven the same talents and tastes, desires and knowledge we had before. If these are not sufficiently pure and good, if our repentance is not heartfelt, then we may not receive all that heaven is meant to hold for us.

What would be the use of spending seventy years here pursuing certain knowledge and goals if, at death, all counts as nothing and we begin our heavenly lives on a different line of thought and study? Practice now. The more earnestly we follow the studies and duties of our lives of probation, the better fitted we shall be to carry them forward to completion and perfection there.

Several years ago *Guideposts* magazine carried Billy Kay Bothwell's story. She was a high school sophomore and for an English assignment wrote a story called "The Last Week of My Life."

In the paper she told how she would prepare for death if she knew she had one week to live: spending time with her family and friends, visiting the sick and shut-ins with her minister, spending time in the woods enjoying God's beautiful creation and going to church on Sunday.

The paper was dated March 15. One week later, on March 22, she was killed in a car accident.

Jesus said, "Behold, I am coming quickly, and My reward is with Me" (Revelation 22:12). Now is the time to prepare.

One important rehearsal that I think is fun to invest in here is singing.

I have an old record album of Ethel Waters singing, "When the storms of life are raging, stand by me." Many times when prayer does not lift us out of the day's fog, a sacrifice of singing will.

In December 1985 a skilled surgeon successfully removed an English walnut-sized tumor from down inside my spinal column. The recovery was slow and painful. I am so grateful that I am now free from pain and able to walk from three to five miles a day.

I was not prepared, however, for what is known as "post-surgical letdown." When people used to tell me about depression I did not understand the term. I do now. About five weeks after surgery a heavy, dark blanket descended on me and I could not lift it. I prayed. I walked the floor. I read the Psalms out loud. I was living in North Dakota and went outside in the zero temperatures to freeze it to death, but that unexplainable dark atmosphere squelched me down, down.

Then one day I sat at the piano. My fingers would hardly move, my mind would hardly perform. The words came from a weak, feeble voice, scratchy and helpless, but I sacrificed a song of praise. I sang, "Praise the name of Jesus, praise the name of Jesus. . . ."

Each verse got stronger. I began to feel elevated, like climbing a ladder one step at a time, up and out of the pit until I could see the light and feel the sun on my spirit's face!

Even if you cannot sing well, begin worshiping God in song, rehearsing for the time when you will join that grand chorus and give Him praise for redeeming you out of sorrow into His glorious forever.

George Herbert (1593–1633) wrote of praising God:

> Seven whole days, not one in seven, I will praise thee;
> in my heart, though not in heaven, I can raise thee.
> Small it is, in this poor sort to enroll thee:
> e'en eternity's too short to extol thee.

This morning at about ten before seven, the sun was coming up with a rosy glow and the mockingbirds in the holly bushes by my bedroom window were rehearsing, singing. I woke with a song in my heart, too, practicing for church this morning and for eternity where I will sing the way I have always wanted to sing.

I was born with a girl's body but a low, boy's singing voice. Nevertheless, I could sing fairly well until I had five nodes removed from my voice box. My voice does not sound as good as it did before surgery, but during my death experience I stood by the gates and joined the singers, and I sang as I feel it in my heart. That is one of the reasons I believe we will be able to do there what we have yearned to do here. We will be standing in the source of music and joy.

This completeness in us will extend even to areas of personality that we are working on as a sort of rehearsal for heaven. I am learning, for instance, to control my short fuse. I tend to pop off quickly. I have a Scripture verse pasted on my mirror: "Set a watch, O LORD, before my mouth; keep the door of my lips" (Psalm 141:3, KJV). There I will finally *be* good and will desire only good things.

It is amazing how some of things we focus on briefly here, things like singing or building character, will be important there, and some things we think are so important here, certain cravings, will be without consequence there.

I was sitting in the Minneapolis airport some years ago when an attractive young woman offered me a cigarette.

"No thanks," I replied. "I'm too stingy to smoke. Too proud, too; don't want my breath bad or my teeth yellow." Then I laughed.

She smiled in return. "Oh, I see. I thought you were going to be like my mom and preach at me. Tell me," she said. "Give me one good reason why I shouldn't smoke."

I thought to myself, *I've already given you two!* But out loud I said, "I guess that sign says it all." I pointed to the letters that stood out above the jetway door: No *Smoking Beyond.*

She laughed and said, "If I can't smoke in heaven I guess I won't go! I'm telling you the same as I told the doctor when I went to get something for my cough. I'd rather die than quit cigarettes."

Now I certainly do not advocate smoking, but bad habits— even for someone as addicted as that young woman—will be so insignificant that once you step into that glorious place, you will never think of them again. "Old things are passed away; behold, all things are become new" (2 Corinthians 5:17, KJV). This is a Scripture promise for the new believer here, and it pertains to the new arrival there, too. I believe that some self-indulgence we think we cannot live without here will be discarded like a menstrual pad.

Pray for an understanding heart to help people along the way to overcome sin and discard their hang-ups. Pray to become intensely spiritual that you may become genuinely human. Exhort the weak along the road. The angels are strong to minister because they worship and bless and obey God. We humans can have supernatural strength if we follow their example along our journey. We have the power of life and death in our tongues (see Proverbs 18.21). There are no dead words.

Not long ago I saw the movie *Cross Creek* about Marjorie Kinnan Rawlings, a Florida writer and author of *The Yearling.* She loved the sky, the water, the earth. She said, "I was a part of the earth before I became a part of the womb."

We were created from the earth, belong to time and are headed for eternity!

Several years ago, when I first started writing, I cried mother tears while I interviewed a young fellow who had just broken both wrists during a basketball game. Looking up at his mother and me with a big smile, he cheered, "We won!"

What a victory cry we will give when we stand at those gates knowing we have given it our all, we have rehearsed and are now ready. "We made it!" we will shout. "We won!"

In the words of this old Gospel song:

> I am watching for the coming of the glad millennial day,
> When our blessed Lord shall come and catch His wait-
>   ing Bride away;
> Oh! my heart is fill'd with rapture as I labor, watch and
>   pray,
> For our Lord is coming back to earth again.
>
> James M. Kirk (1854–1945)

9

All Things New

$\mathbf{M}$any jokes come to me through my mailbox, a number of them bantering about St. Peter at the heavenly gates screening applicants. One man wrote: "There is no prejudice there. Here's all it takes to get in: The Catholics just have to spell God, and the Protestants just have to spell Albuquerque."

In one sense heaven is found very easily: by believing in Jesus Christ.

In another sense this is not so easy because it means giving yourself to Him totally, allowing yourself forevermore to be under His Lordship and sovereignty. Yet you will never find a kinder or truer Master. And you will find no other way to heaven but by believing on His name. Entrance to heaven is not acquired by our works or accomplishments, lest we would be able to boast about ourselves. It is given as a free gift of grace in response to a heart of faith (see Ephesians 2:8–9).

Jesus came to show us how to live life. He said that His yoke was easy, His burden light. He never hurried, never worried. He lived with the answer because He was the answer. Many churches have complicated Christianity. They have become as practical to eternal life as a silk hat in a hurricane or a clown at a funeral. Some have become religious theaters, drama centers. They offer something more akin to rehearsed religion than reality where a person can simply find the door to eternal life and be born again.

The Lord draws us back regularly to simplicity. We must avoid the superficial, the fads.

Just as you can have only one earthly father, there is only one way to your heavenly Father, and that is through Jesus. The same rule applies for getting through life as getting through Mammoth Cave: Stay close to your guide. Jesus' life was not a performance but a process, as ours should be.

We must resolve that our churches are not Hollywood and our leaders are not movie stars. People struggling for security, survival and salvation will look to us if we are real, if we are sincere.

Jesus spent a great deal of time teaching how we must become like little children if we are to inherit the Kingdom of God. I love the fable *The Little Prince* by Antoine de Saint-Exupery. The little prince asks a question and the Answerer replies hurriedly, "No, I don't believe anything. I answered you with the first thing that came into my head. Don't you see—I am very busy with matters of consequence."

The little prince stared. "Matters of consequence? You talk just like the grown-ups!"

For heaven's sake, quit acting like an adult!

I spoke once at a Lutheran Conference on the Holy Spirit in Madison, Wisconsin. It was held in a Roman Catholic convent, and I stayed in one of the sisters' rooms. The floor was plain tile; no carpet. There was a chest, a desk, a twin-sized bed and no mirror. You would be surprised how much time we could save if there were no mirrors! We would not worry so much about how we look, just how we feel. The idea was that those women were there for one purpose: learning how to get people to heaven.

John Sherrill, although a religion writer, confessed how years ago he finally realized that the people who were busiest with religion were sometimes farthest from the real, life-changing heart of it—himself included. One day, while facing cancer surgery, he removed the roadblocks of logic and quit approaching Jesus with his mind. Suddenly he said out loud, "I'm making the leap by faith. I believe in Jesus." His life was never the same again.

Personally, I believe that after being born again, after Jesus' blood has washed away our sins of the past, we should at the first opportunity be baptized. This is the public confession of the personal inward work of grace. Some of my family have been baptized inside the sanctuary of the church, but, since Jesus was baptized in a river, I asked to be baptized outside by immersion. Baptism is a symbol that represents Jesus' death, burial and resurrection. It represents that fact that we were dead in trespasses and sins and have buried the old life and risen to walk a new life.

Perhaps you are reading this now and you have been baptized and confirmed, but were in such a hurry you did not receive all that God intended you to have. Pause and believe. Trust and receive with childlike faith. Jesus said that unless we receive the Kingdom of God as a little child we shall not enter in (see Mark 10:15).

There is nothing quite like the faith—or imagination—of a child! I have received letters from children who are excited about heaven, but worried about how they will get there, especially if they are taken up in the Rapture. They imagine dangling up in the sky or floating along without a good foothold.

I write back to tell them that death or the Rapture will happen as quickly as the lightning flashes from the east to the west (see Matthew 24:27) or as quick as a wink (see 1 Corinthians 15:52). Jesus will come and take us so fast we will not know it has happened until we are suddenly there. It is just like the way we cannot detect the exact second we fall asleep at night; it is that quick.

The Bible says that during the Rapture two will be sleeping in one bed; one will be taken, the other left. It will happen before they even realize it. Likewise, two will be working the field, and the one who is ready will be taken and the other will not. I can just see a Dakota tractor go into automatic pilot when some good man takes off for heaven!

Evelyn Pacadio wrote me about a dream she had of quick transport to heaven. She saw her family in transportation with wheels whirring rapidly. She believes these are the wheels spoken of in Ezekiel, and that Jesus is represented by the wheel in the middle of a wheel.

I believe it is possible to decide how you depart: It is according to the way you have lived. I want to tell you about our old friend Noel Perkin. He was national missions secretary/treasurer for the General Council of the Assemblies of God for many years. My maiden name was Perkins and he used to tease me, an unknown, that my name had the *s* for distinction. He was that modest in everything he did. A big man can afford to be magnanimous.

One Sunday I was embarrassed to arrive late for the church services. I was slipping into the children's church entrance when I caught sight of Noel Perkin arriving late, too. He patted my back and, grinning, said, "Now that the saints are all seated, shall *we* go in?"

Noel was more than ninety years old when his time came. He told our friend Gary McGee that he was going to die on Wednesday. "I have prayed that the Lord not take me at home," he said, "since my wife is in a wheelchair and would feel helpless to assist me and would have bad memories in our house."

On Wednesday morning he knelt beside his bed, read a passage from his Bible, underlined it and left a note that they should use it for his funeral. He then left the house to go make some hospital visitations. He opened the car door and, perhaps feeling faint, knelt and laid his head on his arms on the front seat. Then he simply slept. What a way to go!

Ann Moreton was an airline hostess married to a florist. Fred was suffering with an inoperable malignancy. He prayed, "Lord, I want to die in dignity." He had lived that way, reading his Bible, giving away lots of flowers, so why not?

Ann was leaving the hospital one evening when he told her, "Go home and get a nap. Be sure you come back by midnight."

That evening she was at home and started to write some letters when suddenly she felt two hands on her shoulders pushing her in the direction of the door. She followed the nudge and hurried to the hospital. There she greeted him. "Hello, Freddie. I've come to stay with you."

"That's fine, sweetie," he said in a natural tone of voice, "for I'm dying."

He breathed a few shallow breaths, then said, "God, I'm coming." It was over easily. Ann said that everything in the room appeared to be in "soft focus."

Fred's spirit had grown too large for his earth body. The doctors said, "We've never seen anyone go in such an open, clear eyed way."

Ann said that after seeing him suffer for two years all she could do was lay her head down on the table and rest.

Bobbie Morrison's mother was dying of cancer. Bobbie was with her mother when she said, "Jesus is at the door. Let Him in." Bobbie could tell by the look on her mother's face that she really saw something. Though Bobbie could not detect anything unusual she said she knew by the atmosphere in the room that they were not alone.

Bobbie hugged her mother and said, "Don't leave me now that we're just getting to know each other."

Her mother said, "I have to go." And she did so, totally unafraid. Thank God for His eternal plan in which we can redeem the time lost on earth.

Coni Perez wrote this from Los Angeles:

My three sisters and I all felt compelled at the same time to visit my mother's hospital room. I knew she was dying when we arrived. I prayed that the Lord would send angels to attend her and make it easy for her. We suddenly felt an unbelievable power in the room. The solid line appeared on her heart monitor, then her eyes were open again. She ooohed at the wonders she was seeing, cocked her head to one side as if in extreme attention, smiled the greatest, grandest, broadest smile, lifted both arms straight upward and was gone.

The time is drawing near when the angels will shout and sing, "Hallelujah! The Lord omnipotent reigneth!" I think that the Lord will invite us to a royal banquet given by Himself in honor of the last arrivals. I can hardly wait to sing the Doxology— "Praise God from whom all blessings flow. . . ." I can just see the many rows of banquet tables, covered in white linen, gorgeously furnished with golden plates and crystal stemware, fruits from the Tree of Life served by angelic waiters. We will lack nothing.

I believe we will have dinner music sung by special singers from earth and perhaps violinists strolling by, great musicians hitting perfect pitch. No untuned strings, no self-consciousness, everyone doing his or her best for Him and us.

Perhaps David the psalmist will stand and sing from the book of Revelation: "God shall wipe away all tears from their eyes; and there shall be no more death, neither sorrow, nor crying, neither shall there be any more pain: for the former things are passed away" (Revelation 21:4, KJV)

And He that sits upon the throne may stand and announce:

"Behold, I am making all things new. . . . I am the Alpha and the Omega, the beginning and the end. I will give to the one who thirsts from the spring of the water of life without cost. He who overcomes shall inherit these things, and I will be his God and he will be My son."

Revelation 21:5–7

Then we will shout, "Hallelujah!"

Daniel may be sitting next to you and lean over and whisper, "What a moment this is for me! While I was on earth I saw Him as the Ancient of Days long before His Advent in the womb of the Virgin Mary. His garment was white as snow and the hair of His head was like pure wool. In the revelations God gave me I saw Him sitting on that very throne. Look, His throne is like a fiery flame. He is now Judge and the books are finally opening."

All things will be made new, and we can be there to see them. If you have found the way, do not let anything cause you to stray from the course. There is no greater treasure on this earth than the pathway to heaven. And if you remain faithful, He will look at you at the end of it with the light of His love and say, "Welcome!"

10

The Banking System of Eternity

Every creature, I believe, is born with the desire not only to survive but to thrive.

Perhaps I think this because of the games my Aunt Pearl, whom I then called Pib, and I used to play. Since we were close in age, and since we grew up before the days of television, we made up games and played "pretend" all day long, usually having to do with lives of luxury.

We would place two chairs on the flat-top roof of my grandparents' cow shed and sit up there dressed regally in high heels, purses with wads of play money and plastic jewelry, and pretend to reign as British royalty. We were queens over our domain, which was three acres including a blackberry patch, a cornfield, a ditch, a creek, a cow and a calf, and a grape arbor. Dad Burns' old Ford was our limousine.

At school we skipped rope while singing, "Rich man, poor man, beggar man, thief, doctor, lawyer, merchant, chief." The word you were saying when you missed indicated the profession of the man you would marry. Naturally, we were not disappointed when "rich man" was the choice!

In the midst of this fanciful living, faith was instilled in us from the bassinet during "family altar" and daily devotions. We had faith to believe that God would give us anything we asked, and actually prayed that our dolls would come to life. When our dolls did not start breathing, we put mustard in their diapers and mothered them nonetheless. I am glad God reserves the answers to some prayers for a more appropriate time. At age ten we were not quite prepared for motherhood!

Through the years Pearl and I have overcome many hurdles and faced many storms, and have found God faithful. Our childhood dreams of riches have changed into the longing for the inheritance waiting for us in heaven. It is there that all of our dreams will come true. The investments in the Bank of Eternity will meet every need and every desire.

How do we determine what inheritances are waiting for each of us? How do we transfer funds into eternity's bank? How do we get assets from planet earth to planet heaven?

Our shares in the Bank of Eternity are based on the investments we make while living here on earth. And the best way to make investments into our heavenly accounts is by investing in others. When someone gives to others in this life in the name of Jesus, it is like putting it into the Lord's hand to invest—not for 5.25 percent, but 100 percent! One hundredfold! Even one cup of water, given in His name, will transfer for great yield of reward there.

Jesus explained how our service here reaps rewards there when He said that the one who would be the greatest must serve (see Matthew 23:11). The Bible also says that believers will receive crowns, which will be converted to positions of rulership. By serving in a humble and lowly fashion here, we will rule with Christ in eternity.

I received a professionally printed appeal from a male hairstylist begging me to contribute one thousand dollars so he could enter a contest in France. That same day I got a letter from a retired couple, he a minister, she a nurse, asking the name of a young woman I had told them about who had cancer. They wanted to offer her a home, care, love and medical ministry—in effect, to become the parents she did not have. What a contrast!

If the hairstylist makes it to heaven, his halo will outshine his hairdo, but that couple is investing in a person who will live as a witness to their love forever.

Ralph Wilkerson tells of a missionary friend of his who built several churches in the Philippines. One of his first was in Manila in a huge evangelistic center able to accommodate thousands. Then God called him into the bush. How did he set about to introduce the pagans to Christ?

First he built his house on a path where a tribe passed regularly going to the springs for water. He tried preaching, but got no response. Then he decided to quit preaching and start "practicing Jesus." The next day when an elderly man came by he gave him a cup of water from his well and said simply, "I give you this drink in Jesus' name."

Before long, more of the tribesmen were stopping for the free water. Soon they were not just drinking natural water, but the Water of Life, Christ. Now the tribe is coming to know Jesus.

People do not care how much you know until they know how much you care.

I have made it a practice to invest in people anonymously as much as possible. It is fun to give this way in the name of the Lord and, most important, God is honored. Remember that those recording angels are excellent bookkeepers and gauge your motive as much as your gift. Am I doing it through love or to show off my goodness, my charity, my "spirituality," my wealth?

God says He "is not unjust so as to forget [our] works and the love [we] have shown toward His name, in . . . ministering to the saints" (Hebrews 6:10). And we know that where our treasure is, our heart will be also (see Luke 12:34). If we throw our hearts into serving Jesus, eventually our bodies will follow our treasures to heaven.

Some people's main talent seems to be making money. This is meant to be a means of service, stewardship of what God has given them. Still, it is not merely the amount that one gives that matters, but one's attitude.

My grandparents rented a house on a hillside west of Terre Haute for sixty years. They rented it most of those years from a miserly landlady. She complained that her husband would eat a whole potato if she would fix it for him. She died alone of malnutrition with $1,800 under her mattress, too stingy to pay someone to go and do her grocery shopping for her.

Dr. Arnot gives this apt illustration regarding our lives and eternity's treasure. A ship bearing a company of immigrants is driven off-course and wrecked on an island. They have a good stock of food, plenty of seed, fine soil, and spring and summer ahead of them.

Before plans are made to fell trees and plant crops, they explore and find a gold mine. They begin to dig right away and to labor day after day and month after month. They acquire great heaps of gold, but spring is now past and not a field has been cleared, not a grain of seed put into the ground.

Summer comes and their wealth increases, but the stock of food grows small. Soon they are eating the seed. In the fall they find that their heaps of gold are worthless in the face of famine.

They rush to fell trees, till the ground and sow the seed, but it is too late. Winter has come and the seed rots in the ground. They die of want in the midst of their treasure.

This earth is like that island, with eternity the ocean around it. On this shore we have the living seed, but we are constantly enticed to spend our time and energy elsewhere. Once winter overtakes us in our useless toil, however, we are without the

Bread of Life and are lost. As Christians we should value all the more the home that holds the treasure we desire and should remember that we invest in eternity by the way we live now.

Ministers would not have to urge people to live for heaven if their treasures were up there; their hearts would already be there.

I talked with a former prostitute from a southern city in the United States. She said, "I made a lot of money by evil. Now that God has redeemed me through Jesus I have transferred my funds into the hands of the preachers I used to hate as religious fanatics." Your money goes where your heart is.

Mrs. William Booth, co-founder with her husband of The Salvation Army, told her daughter, "The moments of opportunity here will be worth countless millions there. The inestimable privileges of time will make us ashamed that we did not take heaven's banking system more seriously."

Peter said that those who remain sure of their calling will have "the entrance into the eternal kingdom of our Lord and Savior Jesus Christ . . . abundantly supplied" (2 Peter 1:10–11).

When Carl's first wife died, he asked that in lieu of flowers that would wither, gifts of money be given to their daughter, Connie, so she could go to Bible school. Now with that love gift and a grant, she is doing just that. The going was not always easy, but she persevered through the difficult times and is enjoying her reward.

We might think of this earth as college training for the forever life. "So teach us to number our days, that we may apply our hearts unto wisdom" (Psalm 90:12, KJV).

Who knows the wealth and position for which God is preparing us? Even if He is subjecting us to painful training now, we should not rebel. His plans are always good and every adversity we face will be used to help prepare us for eternity with Him. The more we are able to overcome our trials with grace and humility, the more we will find waiting for us in eternity's bank.

God has always had a remnant throughout the centuries willing to pay the price of spiritual maturity. As a man seeks treasure, so the Lord seeks followers like these. "For the eyes of the LORD run to and fro throughout the whole earth, to shew himself strong in the behalf of them whose heart is perfect toward him" (2 Chronicles 16:9, KJV).

We will find that the wealthy ones in heaven were first servants here on earth (see Mark 10:43–44). They are the ones who give their time to fold stacks of Sunday school papers or tend to the church nursery or chauffeur the elderly. The quiet person of prayer will likely be met with a twenty-piece angelic brass band, while some who have been showier in their approaches to Christianity will be less heralded. We forget some of the little things we have done, but they are all recorded, and rewards are waiting for us. If our small deeds are rewarded, what might the benefit be for larger sacrifices?

Do not miss these rewards at any cost, for they must be wonderful. In the book of Revelation Jesus says, "He who overcomes, I will grant to him to sit down with Me on My throne, as I also overcame and sat down with My Father on His throne" (Revelation 3:21).

Now is the time to give our best. Attain our highest for Him here with all diligence. Work hard. Make every effort for others. Be earnest. "Those who have insight will shine brightly like the brightness of the expanse of heaven, and those who lead the many to righteousness, like the stars forever and ever" (Daniel 12:3).

All who believe in Jesus will go to heaven, but as I understand it we will be assigned to different locations or planes. Just as "star differs from star in glory" (1 Corinthians 15:41), all will have mansions, but some will be grander than others. All will serve, but some in higher positions according to their obedience on earth. All will be happy, but some will be happier.

If only we could understand the glories of heaven we would lead very different lives, seeking to be ready for it. Our imaginations cannot fathom even a small part of how grand and real heaven is.

When the steamship *Central America* went down in 1857, several hundred miners, returning with fortunes in gold, lost their lives. There is nothing wrong with having gold, but it makes a bad life-preserver. Riches can be a weight that crushes us down to hell, that drowns us in the sea of life.

As John Milton said, there is nothing that makes men rich and strong but that which they carry inside of them. True wealth is of the heart, not of the hand.

Make yourself a private inventory sheet and list your goals. How many of them are spiritual, eternal goals and how many are temporary, material goals? This may help you see how much you are investing in the Bank of Heaven.

Look at the story Jesus told of the rich man and Lazarus. The rich man looks over his marble balcony at Lazarus the beggar and commands his dogs, "Take hold of him."

The dogs start at the beggar with a terrible snarl, then they stop and yawn. They frisk about him and put their soft, healing tongues to his sores, driving away the flies, relieving the sting of wounds that have no salve or bandage. Lazarus is friends with the rich man's dogs.

Then Lazarus dies. Two men dig a hole and lower him into a pauper's grave. But it isn't Lazarus they bury. It is only his sores. Yonder goes Lazarus with an angel on the right and an angel on the left. They carry him to heaven, talking, praising and rejoicing.

Abraham stands at the gate and throws his arms around the newcomer. Lazarus has his own house, his own robes, his own banquet table and chariot; and that poor sickly carcass of his that the overseers of the town dumped in the potter's field will come up at the call of the archangel straight and pure and healthy, corruption having become incorruption.

Now, back in the city, the dead body of the rich man lies in state in an expensive coffin placed on an Oriental rug. He is carried out of his splendid room through the streets where long eulogies are given. A long procession files to his burial place.

The rich man who had all the wines he could drink now asks for plainer beverage: He just wants water. Not a cupful, not a teaspoonful, but just "one drop" and he cannot get it. He looks and sees Lazarus, the object of his animosity, resting joyfully with Abraham.

He calls to the patriarch and begs for Lazarus to put his finger in water and let him lick it off. Once Lazarus asked for crumbs from his feast; now the rich man begs for a drop of water from Lazarus' banquet.

Poor as he can be, the rich man has eaten his last quail wing. He has broken the last rind of his last pomegranate. The rich lord has become the pauper. Now he sits at the gate, watching the heavenly festivities with longing.

The social gulf that separated Lazarus from the rich man in this world is not nearly as great as the spiritual chasm that now separates them forever. He begs Abraham to send Lazarus to his brothers to warn them before it is too late for them, too.

But as Abraham tells him, most people are preoccupied with their comforts, and even if someone did come back from the dead (and people have) they would not listen.

Jesus did not by this parable condemn the acquisition of wealth, but its wrongful application. A man of wealth is not necessarily a sinner. Solomon and David were both rich, as was Job. And we are glad for the great philanthropists who give their gifts to colleges, churches and hospitals for education, ministry and relief for the poor.

Jesus had in mind the haughty, vain and self-sufficient rich who, like the Pharisees, use their wealth to oppress the less fortunate and to make a vulgar show of their advantages. It is this pride, pomp and circumstance that leads their hearts away from God.

Jesus is the Messiah and will return for His believers to take them to His heavenly Kingdom. He said that many would try to show us signs of His appearing, but to regard none of them, for they are intended to catch the weak and lead them to destruction.

When the Son of Man comes in judgment it will be sudden like lightning. Just as it was in the days of Noah when the floods came to swallow up the world after the people refused to repent of their perversions, just as it was when Sodom was consumed for its offenses, so will it be again when Jesus comes and reveals His power.

In that day, those who have not prepared themselves, as did Noah and Lot by prayer and repentance, will be destroyed. The good in family, social and business relations will be separated from the bad. The evil will be delivered up for punishment; the righteous will go to their reward.

How can you multiply your investments in heaven's bank? Give to the poor. Do not be high-minded or trust in riches. Do good works. Build for yourself a trust fund in heaven and you will find that He helps you out here on earth, too. God often advances to His people on earth some of the interest they are earning on their eternal benefits—with the principal still intact in the Bank of Eternity. Some of these assets are love, peace, joy, eternal youth and energy, forever life. Scripture says to give and it will be given to you, good measure, pressed down, shaken together and running over (see Luke 6:38). And that is just for starters! The principal that is building and the interest that is accruing are awaiting your arrival in heaven.

It seems that we *can* take it with us! Everything we give away we keep. We are converting it into heavenly currency, exchanging paper money for wealth that cannot burn or fade. "The generous man will be prosperous, and he who waters will himself be watered. . . . He who trusts in his riches will fall" (Proverbs 11:25, 28) or as the King James Version puts it: "There is that with-holdeth more than is meet, but it tendeth to poverty. The liberal soul shall be made fat" (verses 24–25).

If you want a sure investment, ask the Lord in private prayer what you can do this week for the church or someone in need!

11

What Is Forever For?

You have undoubtedly heard expressions like *You mean there's more?* and *I never dreamed that . . .* and *Have you ever . . . ?*

Upon our arrival at heaven's golden shore I am sure we will exclaim that we had no idea there could be so much more to living, that we had only begun to know the rudiments of life at its fullest and living at its best, that there is more than we had ever imagined.

I cannot wait to introduce John to our daughter April. If the Rapture occurs before I die I hope the Lord will cause me to zigzag a little on the way up to meet Erika and Ryan, our grandchildren, and meet John with one on each hand! Then I want to walk over to my mother and let her see her great-grandchildren.

Carl feels the same way. His grandchildren are scattered from North Dakota to North Carolina. We will have plenty of time there to play with our grandchildren.

Have you ever wondered what we will do for all of eternity? I can assure you there will be no monotony in heaven. There will also be no pressure, because we will not sense the passing of time. It will be impossible for us to fail. Everything we touch will succeed.

My dad says he wants forever to make up to Mother for the years on earth that he expected too much of her. She was never strong and died young trying to please everyone as mother, wife, pianist, teacher, even substitute preacher when he had to miss church for some reason.

I imagine that any writer who has ever received a rejection slip will want to visit the "Acceptance Department"!

Many performers will be in the spotlight on heaven's "Request Night." Remember camp meeting when you could never get enough of the good singing? I think I will request that Gordon Matheny and the Paino Brothers sing their old numbers "Looking for a City" and "The Stone Hewn Out of the Mountain."

Maybe you have always wanted to learn to play a piano yourself, or a harp. If you so desire, you could probably sign up for music lessons from King David or Bach. They will have plenty of time, forever, in fact, to teach and you to learn. There will be no lack of talent there, either. That place will lack nothing.

Carl will sign up for classes with St. Paul in biblical studies and church history.

And women will finally receive deserved recognition for their giftings. Generations past have not always acknowledged the talents of women. I believe that God passes out talent without stopping to examine sex organs to see if the person is male or female.

My daughter Brenda is a music major and teaches piano. She is conscientious about copyrights and giving credit to whom credit is due. Recently she wrote me about some new music she had tracked down:

> You're familiar with the composer Robert Schumann. It seems that his wife, Clara, was a composer, too. Before she married

126

she was considered one of the world's greatest pianists and did a lot of composing herself. (Chopin asked her to perform his music because she did it better than anyone else.) She wrote only a few things during her marriage, and Robert was critical of most of it. She bore him eight children (five of whom lived) and edited most of his compositions. When he died she taught piano lessons and her mother helped her raise the children.

I also picked up a collection of compositions by Mendelssohn's sister Fanny. Musicologists are starting to think that Fanny wrote some of what her brother published under his own name, for example, some of his *Songs without Words*.

Any mistreatment will be compensated for, and all other records—good and bad—will be accurate for forever. There is no prejudice among angels. What a relief!

It is amazing when traveling how often I deplane to comments or questions about bad news around the country. I like to smile and answer, "I stand behind not the Fifth Amendment but Philippians 4:8: Whatsoever things are lovely, of *good* report, think on these things."

Are you glad, as I am, that there will be no more gory news details on TV at 5:30 every afternoon? (I have often concluded that if Jesus comes at 5:40 my husband might miss the Rapture!)

There will be no misunderstandings there. I have tried to adopt my grandfather's definition of *maturity*: Suffer without complaining; be misunderstood without explaining. That is hard, but the records will be straightened out there. We will have our day in court.

I saw a vivid example one Sunday morning when I was quite small of how we can misjudge our fellowman. This was before cars had automatic turn signals; you used your left arm.

Dad was driving our old Hudson. We were running late for church and the man in front of us was driving quite slowly. Then he turned quickly to the left without signaling in order to get a newspaper from a boy barking "Sunday *News*!" on the corner.

As Dad braked to a halt, he remarked, "He could have caused a wreck! How did he ever get a license without learning hand signals?"

When the man stepped out of his car, we saw that the sleeve on the left side of his shirt covered only a stump of an arm. My father was quite chagrined to have judged him, and I learned a valuable lesson.

Last week Carl and I took a break from work and headed for the beach for an hour. We saw an older woman trying to cross the street holding a bag. She slid on a rock, turned her ankle and flung apples all along the curb. Carl stopped the car, and I ran over to help her out of the traffic.

She hung onto my neck and asked pitifully, "Is this what *old* means?" I had to tell her that it happens to us all here, but there is no "old" in heaven. She cried and replied, "Then let's go there."

We will have forever for joys and accomplishments.

I believe we will have total recall, no mental limitations. I have read that we use only about 10 percent of the brain's capacity. Everything there will be 100 percent. John 14:26 promises that the Holy Spirit will teach us all things and bring all things to our remembrance.

There will be no power failure in heaven to wipe out a morning's work on your word processor during hurricane season. No tornadoes, either.

The thief on the cross believed in Jesus at the last minute. The Lord did not have time to teach him anything, but assured him, "Today you will be with Me in Paradise." That man will have forever to learn about Jesus and to enjoy heaven.

If you want a head start, read the Bible—and start singing meaningful songs. It is certain we will not be bored there, sitting around twirling halos like hula hoops. What job opportunities to teach the newcomers! Have you tried to tell someone something who already knows everything? I hate to try to feed a kid who is not hungry. I want to teach people who have not heard it all, those unspoiled, thirsty learners.

What fun to see relatives we have not seen in ages, and those our parents talked about but we were born too late to know! I have always wanted to meet several Bible characters. I want to know what Samson saw in Delilah that caused him to sell his strength. I want to talk to Jonah about being in that whale's stomach.

I will not be afraid of breaking my neck when I learn to water ski on just one ski. I might even walk on the water. Scripture tells us that the River of Life is a sea like glass. There is no drowning, no death, no risk involved.

There will be no more worrying about the affairs of the nations, either. The destiny of the universe, including the planet earth, will be under the jurisdiction of God from His throne in heaven. Romans 13:1 says that "the powers that be are ordained of God" (KJV). Daniel 2:21 says that God removes kings and sets up kings.

I am looking forward to being free from worry about my children. Mother used to say that when your children are babies you worry about their safety. When they are growing up your worry increases as you watch them learn to drive and start dating. When they marry you worry about their being properly respected. When they are safely adjusted in their marriages you worry about the inexperienced way they rear your grandchildren!

Even though I pray the Scripture "I know whom I have believed and am persuaded that he is able to keep that which I have committed unto him against *that day*," I still have a tender, overconcerned heart. I promised John I would bring them "home" to him.

Judy Provost wrote me from California, "I have just lost my partner. We had such a good life. We loved taking walks by the ocean. I can't believe it's over."

It isn't. Those hikes will be continued in a lovelier place. I have been to California and to heaven and, believe me, the most beautiful part of California—or anywhere else—is shabby by comparison.

Uncle Arch Brown, my great-uncle, used to sing this old Gospel song:

> When I take my vacation in heaven,
> What a wonderful time that will be—
> Hearing concerts by the heavenly chorus,
> And the face of my Savior I'll see.
>
> Sitting down by the banks of the river
> 'Neath the shade of the evergreen tree
> I shall rest from my burdens forever,
> Won't you spend your vacation with me?
> Herbert Buffum (1879–1939) and
> R. E. Winsett (1876–1952)

If you want to travel, that is what forever is for. Read the description of the Garden of Eden. This was a transplant from the original Paradise. Can you imagine touring cliffs, mountains, vales and glens? The fields will be teeming with harvest, the valleys spread out before you.

Not a drop of sweat will be needed to gather these fields of golden harvest. No curse there, no weeds, thorns or briars. Everything grows in heaven without human toil. We will be employed to gather the great harvests, and that labor will be a kind of picnic for joy.

There will be plenty of room for the millions who are born again and come there with hope, joy, expectation. I have fond memories of drinking from the unpolluted streams of North and South Dakota right after the snows melted. What *cooool* refreshment! Think of drinking from the river proceeding out of the throne of God. You could dip a golden goblet into it, drink and never thirst again. How invigorating it will be after drinking water from the River of Life to feel the joyful glow of youth—never to feel tired, weary or old again!

I believe that we can go from place to place either in the air or along the solid foundations of the celestial country. "There the glorious LORD will be unto us a place of broad rivers and streams; wherein shall go no galley with oars" (Isaiah 33:21, KJV). Can you imagine a boat ride powered by the Holy Spirit's energy—no noisy motors, but heaven's boost of light and power? Perhaps on the shore can be heard angelic groups singing and praising God night and day.

I believe we will hear old and new songs. I think that many of the inspired songs we hear now on earth were inspired first in heaven, and we will sing them there. There will be concerts perhaps daily, and the Temple will be "filled with smoke from the glory of God and from His power" (Revelation 15:8). Trumpeters will play and hosts sing:

> Holy, holy, holy! Lord God Almighty!
> All Thy works shall praise Thy Name, in earth, and sky, and sea;
> Holy, holy, holy, merciful and mighty!
> God in Three Persons, blessed Trinity!
> Reginald Heber (1783–1826)

We will never tire of study. Much will be taught just by observation as we take in at our leisure all the parts of His heavenly Kingdom.

We will never lack for social pleasures and enjoyments for there is no clashing of duty with inclination, no unfulfilled desires, no vain striving for the unattainable in that life.

I would not be surprised if some of us whose friends or relatives were builders find that they have built us a home on the water, if we like water sports, with bluebirds singing in the overhanging willow nearby and hummingbirds darting in and out of the flowery window boxes.

Many precious hours will be spent with our families that we did not have time for before, as we go with each other to our various fields of labor and ministry—particularly helping instruct those who come into the new life with little or no knowledge of the heavenly.

I imagine there will be talks, lectures, sharing times when we can hear Martin Luther, John Wesley, George Whitefield; when we can enjoy the happy presence of the Virgin Mary and hear her tell of the visit by the angel Gabriel and the events that followed. Perhaps we will hear a pep talk (not that we will need it!) from Peter, the energetic one.

And imagine the joy of having the Word, the Bethlehem Baby, the Son of God now walking and talking as Friend with friend. What ecstasy!

At some point we will see Jesus sitting on a white horse. It must be some gallant steed. When He was on earth His disciples borrowed a donkey for Him, but there He will be called by the whole universe Faithful and True (see Revelation 19:11).

Now we know in part. There we will see things as they really are. He may take us on a field trip to show us how to make a rainbow or share the ingredients to form a star.

Here we usually receive an inheritance at the death of someone close to us. There we will have our heavenly Father *and* an inheritance! My earthly dad will be there beside me, too. That is a piece of joy. He will be whistling each morning at five o'clock as he used to on our farm, happy to meet the sunrise, loving his work, thinking about heaven.

We will get there what we lost out on here. I recall the words to another old song: "Leave the unknown future in the Master's hands; whether sad or joyful, Jesus understands."

Look around at people you work with or family members who are not looking for that blessed hope, His return. They are spiritually blind, uninformed of the Good News, crippled with feeble knees that have not bent in prayer for years. They have no faith but I believe we can *give them ours* by praying for them.

Look at the New Testament story of the crippled man who had no strength or faith of his own. Four friends carried him, took off a section of the roof in a crowded house and dropped his cot down into the living room in front of Jesus. That man was actually healed because he borrowed someone else's faith.

We can get more faith if we give ours away because we know the Source! Bring those unbelieving people to Jesus and you will have sheaves to lay at the Master's feet. You will receive your crown and hear Him say, "Well done, thou good and faithful servant."

I was amazed by a story of the servanthood of two women living in India a number of years ago who took in abandoned or orphaned children. One of them, an American who was grieving over a broken engagement, had thrown herself into missionary work.

One day they heard a knock on the door early in the morning. A man was standing there with a little bundle in his arms. He said he had gone to the outer edge of the village where a dung heap served as the toilet for the village when he saw something stir in the leaves by a tree. He brushed the leaves away and found a newborn girl. Girls in that culture were not considered worth keeping.

He asked the two women if they would take the child, and they did. They had ten nursing babies at that time and, as one of the women remarked, "We didn't get much sleep, but our prayer life was incredible."

They reared the girl until she was seven years old and a wealthy couple from New Delhi adopted her.

One day, years later, the two women received a letter from London with a picture of the girl, now grown. She wrote that she was musically talented and her adoptive parents had sent her to the London Conservatory of Music. She became a concert pianist and the picture showed her at tea in Buckingham Palace. Today she is married to an executive and holds Bible studies in her home.

It is a long way from a broken engagement to ministry in India. And it is a long way from a dung heap to Buckingham Palace. But if we let the power of God use us here, we will find that we have all of forever to enjoy His good pleasure.

You may have your passport in order and have your ticket in hand, but to take off you must go to the airport. Scripture recommends that we "not [forsake] the assembling of ourselves together . . . as [we] see the day approaching" (Hebrews 10:25, KJV). Find believers to worship with until He appears.

He is coming again. It is the climax of the entire Bible. We are not talking about just the Rapture; we are talking about His revelation. We are not talking about just meeting Him in the air; we are talking about coming back to the earth to reign with Him. We are not talking about solely His coming for the saints; we are talking about His coming with the saints. We are not talking about His coming to comfort and protect; we are talking about His coming to conquer and rule.

No wonder John exploded with praise at the end of the book of Revelation! No wonder he cried out, "Even so, come, Lord Jesus!"

What is forever for? It is for everything good for a long, long time. And we will enjoy every eternal moment of it.

12

Going Home

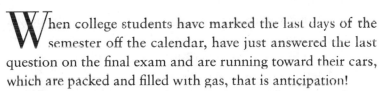

When college students have marked the last days of the semester off the calendar, have just answered the last question on the final exam and are running toward their cars, which are packed and filled with gas, that is anticipation!

Christians have been marking their calendars, too, waiting for the glorious return of Jesus. We will be going home. The Grand Finale.

A book by Sir William Barrett published in 1926 describes many near-death experiences, and the visions of those who died and returned to life. They had many things in common, such as seeing light, grass, feeling an awesome power, hearing music. None, however, reported any signs of building and construction taking place.

In contrast, almost all the reports that I have heard of since 1960 include mention of builders constructing housing for a large number of people apparently expected to arrive at the same time. I believe it is about time for the coming of Christ our King to take us to our inherited home.

In 1960 my family was finally able to realize our dream of moving to Florida. My husband, young daughter and I, along with my mother, dad and two younger brothers, Marvin and Gary, had anticipated it for years, and now it was going to happen.

John and I sold our house and moved into a cramped little gray trailer with Brenda, her dog, her cat and forty dolls. We did not mind being crowded! We were moving to Florida in a few weeks, as soon as the final paperwork was completed on selling my husband's business.

Someone whispered a rumor that we had lost our lovely ranch home and had to sell our business because of bankruptcy. We did not even respond, because we did not really care. It simply did not matter. We knew better. We were moving to Florida! And arriving in Florida was like going home.

We had nine wonderful years before both John and my mother died. I almost lost our home and had to move back to North Dakota with my two small children. But I told my neighbor, "I'll be back. This is home."

I left empty, but once again my dream came true and I came back full. I now have an honorable father for my children, a godly mate. Two years ago as we drove back across the Florida state line I felt as though my heart would burst with the homecoming.

Have no worry about ridicule from unbelievers as you prepare for the journey. Hold on to your dream. We are going home soon! The time for Jesus to come is sooner than it has ever been before.

You may feel burned out, battle-weary, battered, wounded and discouraged. You may have climbed the ladder of success only to find it leaning against the wrong wall. You may be locked into a dead marriage or nursing a dream that has died or fighting pain or sickness. If so, look up! Rejoice, for your redemption draws nigh! If we stand in our shoes of hope on tiptoes of faith, we can see the brightness of His glory (see Ezekiel 1:28–2:1).

We may be troubled on every side, yet we are not distressed. We might be perplexed, but not in despair; persecuted, but not forsaken; cast down, but not destroyed. We have a treasure: the excellence of the power of God. And we know that God who raised Jesus from the dead shall raise us up, too!

An old Russian proverb says that "death takes not the old, but the ripe." It has been harvest time for many. Others may see (or feel!) the law of gravity fail in that Rapture moment when "the trumpet will sound, and the dead will be raised imperishable, and we shall be changed" (1 Corinthians 15:52).

Are you what John Wesley described as an "almost Christian" or are you a prepared Bride, watching and ready? "Let us rejoice and be glad and give the glory to Him, for the marriage of the Lamb has come and His bride has made herself ready" (Revelation 19:7).

Great events are about to occur, among the most interesting that time and eternity have ever known. I believe our Lord has probably alerted the angelic reception committees that the time has nearly arrived when He shall leave the mediatorial throne and, in the company of saints and angels, descend to the earth. We should tell it, write it, impress others with it. The "redemption of the purchased possession" is about to take place. In a short while we will join in singing the song of the Lamb.

If I die before Jesus comes, please refrain from imposing on a church soloist to weep through a mournful song at my funeral. Put on John Hall's tape "Buried Alive" and listen with a smile. One time John Hall and I were on the same television program. I got up out of the makeup chair, flung the apron off my chest and rushed to the door of the television studio in time to hear him say, "The next verse I'm singing is for Betty Malz." How thrilling it was to hear those joyful words: "When they lower these bones down in the ground, I'll be living on the other side!"

The other song I want sung at my funeral is on the tape my lovely friend Lillie Knauls sings: "Finally Home." "But just think of stepping on shore and finding it heaven! . . . Oh, of waking up in Glory, and finding you are home!"

It is no wonder our children in this generation have become confused and frustrated. We keep forgetting to tell them that Jesus is coming again. That is the Good News!

My brother Marvin and his wife, Sharon, were sweethearts from the time they were children about ten years old. I shall always remember their Christmas wedding—and the days leading up to it. Marvin was in Florida and his fiancée in Indiana. He would write and phone to keep in touch. He bought a little four-room house for $5,000 that Mother and I helped him decorate and furnish in Sharon's then-favorite colors of blue and happy orange.

Finally, after the wedding in Indiana, the weariness from two long days of travel vanished from their eyes when he parked in the shell driveway under two little palms he had planted. When he carried her across that humble threshold, they were home.

We want to go home, and Jesus wants us to come. It will not be long. We must not get discouraged and stop waiting for our arrival in our heavenly home. We must not give in to the temptation to believe anything other than what the Bible teaches.

The first lie that Satan used thousands of years ago is same one he uses now. He told Eve, "Eat of this tree and you will be as God." New groups these days, particularly those in the New Age movement, are saying, "There is no heaven, no hell. We will just become wiser and better. We are becoming gods even now."

This worship of ourselves is the epitome of pride and idolatry. That egotism is sharply contrasted with the humility expressed in this legend, which Ed Schlossmacher told in a sermon recently.

Zacchaeus took a walk early each morning. One day his wife decided to follow him and find out where he went. The journey led her to the edge of town to a tree near the road. The tree was old, and Zacchaeus watered it, patted the trunk, hugged that old tree with loving, tender respect.

Why did he nourish that old tree? It was the place where Zacchaeus found Jesus, eternal life, the hope of heaven.

Today go back in your memory to the place where He became life to you. Nothing should get in the way of our love for Him. Hardships in this life are only temporary. Take courage and remember that as soldiers of the cross we are not looking for mansions on the battlefield. A tent will do. We are more concerned with getting the war over and going home.

A few years ago Mary Pallesen came over for a cup of tea. We sat on the sundeck overlooking the Red River Valley area of the prairies of the Dakotas and decided to walk out to Clark's Corner. We failed to contemplate the fact that it was eight miles out—and the same distance back!

I made the mistake of wearing a four-dollar bargain pair of canvas deck shoes without socks. Her gear was not much better. We laughed when Carl suggested we not start out on our first walk with such a big goal, and somehow we actually arrived at Clark's Corner in pretty good repair. Then we turned for home.

There is not much traffic up there on the ridge. We prayed someone would come and pick us up; no one came. The last mile we were sliding our feet along the ground, dragging them in order to move. My left hip felt out of place. My back hurt. We were dehydrated, nearly faint, and my heels had bled so much my shoes were red in the back.

But our pride would not let us quit and our silly sense of humor volleyed back and forth encouraging us to make it. Suddenly we caught sight of the old brown farmhouse with the white gingerbread trim and windowboxes blooming with pink and white petunias! We had made it home! We had succeeded in our venture! We smiled ridiculously between long, gasping drinks of water and collapsed into chairs.

If we took the happiness we felt at that moment of homecoming and magnified it a million times it still could not compare with the exhilaration each of us will feel upon entering the gates of heaven. It seems too good to be true—but it is!

What a homecoming awaits us!

I will see you at the banquet.

Betty Malz was a bestselling author and well-known speaker on the topic of heaven, angels and the supernatural. Her visit to heaven after being declared clinically dead is told in her much-loved *My Glimpse of Eternity*, a book with a foreword by Catherine Marshall that has touched millions of readers since its publication in 1977.

Betty was born in Terre Haute, Indiana, and considered herself a Hoosier through and through. She and her first husband, John Upchurch (who died at age 36), had two daughters, Brenda and April. Her love for Florida led to a move with her second husband, Carl Malz, to the beautiful Florida coast.

A tall, elegant and fun-loving woman, Betty's favorite picture of herself was in her 1962 MGA convertible. She died in February 2012.